Who Cares?

Who Cares?

Life on Welfare in Australia

EVE VINCENT

MELBOURNE
UNIVERSITY
PRESS

MELBOURNE UNIVERSITY PRESS
An imprint of Melbourne University Publishing Limited
Level 1, 715 Swanston Street, Carlton, Victoria 3053, Australia
mup-contact@unimelb.edu.au
www.mup.com.au

First published 2023
Text © Eve Vincent, 2023
Design and typography © Melbourne University Publishing Limited, 2023

This book is copyright. Apart from any use permitted under the *Copyright Act 1968* and subsequent amendments, no part may be reproduced, stored in a retrieval system or transmitted by any means or process whatsoever without the prior written permission of the publishers.

Every attempt has been made to locate the copyright holders for material quoted in this book. Any person or organisation that may have been overlooked or misattributed may contact the publisher.

Cover design by Nada Backovic
Text design and typesetting by Megan Ellis Typesetting
Cover image of cup by Drew Taylor/Unsplash License and rug courtesy the author
Printed in Australia by McPherson's Printing Group

 A catalogue record for this book is available from the National Library of Australia

9780522878950 (paperback)
9780522878967 (ebook)

Contents

Acknowledgements	vii
Preface	ix

Part 1: Welfare mutates

1	Look after them?	3
2	Sustenance	21
3	Surveillance	34

Part 2: Life on welfare

4	'Stressed out to be on the card'	51
5	'Why are you crying? We're here to help you'	73
6	'They think we're rubbish'	93
7	'Had to be done'	110
Afterword: Who cares?		128

Notes	133
References	145
Index	158

Acknowledgements

I owe my deepest gratitude to the many people who appear anonymously in this book. Thank you to every one of you for talking with, trusting and teaching me.

My research into the cashless debit card was supported by the Aboriginal Legal Rights Movement (ALRM). Massive thanks to Lahn Mickan, Billy Haseldine, Kirsty Sansbury and, especially, Marilen Matthews. This book, however, is the outcome of independent research; its contents do not necessarily reflect the views of ALRM.

In Ceduna and in Adelaide many people looked out for me and showed me great generosity. My debts are legion. Since Ceduna is a small town and the card has been an extremely divisive issue, I refrain from listing individuals here. I hope I have conveyed my sincere gratitude in person over the years.

The Council of Single Mothers and their Children (CSMC) and the National Council of Single Mothers and their Children (NCSMC) both supported my research into ParentsNext. I'm very grateful to Andi Sebastian and Terese Edwards. Again, this book does not necessarily reflect the views of CSMC or NCSMC.

My research was funded via a Macquarie University Research Seeding Grant. This book arises from that modest grant: I hope that grants of a similar scale persist into the future. I am thankful for the award of a Macquarie University Publishing Scheme subsidy.

Amid demoralising attacks on universities, I am lucky to have wonderful colleagues at Macquarie. Thanks to Anna-Karina Hermkens, Banu Şenay, Chris Houston, Chris Vasantkumar, Greg Downey, Jaap Timmer and Lisa Wynn. Special thanks to Banu, a treasured friend. Thanks also to Payel Ray, Ben Spies-Butcher and Chris Dixon. Macquarie Master of Research students Gemma Clendining, Taylor Kuper and June Shrestha assisted with the ParentsNext research.

Sister Michele Madigan has my eternal thanks. I am honoured to count Emma Mitchell as a collaborator and friend. I spent a month in 2019 as a visiting fellow at ANU's Centre for Aboriginal Economic Policy Research (CAEPR); thanks to CAEPR colleagues for a warm welcome. Sincere thanks also to Elise Klein.

Parts of this book draw on previously published work. Two publications range over many aspects of the cashless debit card discussed here: 'We've lost our vision: A card cannot give vision to the community', *Inside Story*, 2019, and 'Lived experiences of the cashless debit card trial, Ceduna, South Australia', Centre for Aboriginal Economic Policy Research Working Paper No. 129, 2019. Parts of chapter 6 appear in Emma Mitchell and Eve Vincent, 'The shame of welfare? Lived experiences of welfare and culturally inflected experiences of shame', *Emotion, Space and Society*, 41, 2021, pp. 1–8, as well as 'Paperwork and (im)personalisation effects', *Infrastructural Inequalities*, 2019. Parts of chapters 1 and 7 appear in 'Look after them? Gender, care and welfare reform in Aboriginal Australia', *Ethnos*, 2021.

Thanks to Alison Whittaker for permission to quote from the poem 'ologist', which appears in the brilliant collection *Blakwork*.

I'm thankful to my lovely friends for all the walking, talking, dumplings, road trips and reading room dates: Anna Clark, Anthea Vogl, Camilla Pandolfini, Claire Parfitt, Jemima Mowbray, Jess Whyte, Katie Hepworth, Liz Humphrys, Melinda Hinkson and Rose Butler. Anna, Anthea, Banu, Emma, Jemima, Jess and Melinda all read chapter drafts for me: I'm grateful to them for their insights.

Working with MUP has been a dream. Thanks to Nathan Hollier, Louise Stirling, Cathryn Game and Duncan Fardon. Two anonymous readers' generous feedback improved this manuscript.

The experiences of caregiving related here were closely shared with my amazing sister, Lucy Vincent. Chris Houston was incredibly supportive throughout this period, which made more of a difference than perhaps he realised.

A world of thanks to Shane, Ned and Billy Rose, for all the care given and all the love.

Preface

In early 2020 I began writing this book about life on welfare. I explained that social security in Australia has become more conditional over recent decades as well as more punitive, in concert with a broader global transition. That is, receipt of welfare payments comes with complex conditions attached, and there are financial sanctions associated with non-adherence, or alleged non-adherence, to those conditions. I noted the precipitous decline of the payment rate for unemployed persons, the JobSeeker payment, which was formerly known as Newstart. By then it had eroded to reach a nadir of around $40 per day. To be unemployed meant to subsist in crushing poverty, especially in major Australian cities where housing costs are steep.

My then 12-year-old son was watching the news one summer evening in the 2020 new year: he told me a novel virus had emerged in China. He worries about things. I reassured him, without giving it much thought. 'That won't affect us, Ned.'

In March of that shitty year, I drove to Macquarie University in north-west Sydney where I work. I slowed as I passed through prosperous suburban Ryde. Queues of people stretched out the Centrelink door and along the length of the block.

The unemployment payment rate was effectively doubled in late April 2020 via the 'Coronavirus supplement payment'. The conditions attached to its receipt were temporarily suspended. In the months to come, a Facebook page collected stories about the effect of the extra $550 paid fortnightly. People posted photos of a new heater and bright kids' shoes, bills paid on time, freshly baked banana muffins after the purchase of the ingredients and tray.

Life on welfare had changed, but for how long?

I found myself increasingly busy looking after a beloved aunt. Afflicted with dementia, her brain was atrophying: she needed structure, order and company to slow its disintegration. During the New South Wales 2020 lockdown, my aunt was alone in her house, her routines gone. Every day brought news that was hard to comprehend and bear. Her condition rapidly worsened.

I visited often, and we walked in the Centennial Parklands, drifting through a paperbark grove before looping around glinting blue ponds where fat ducks ruffled their plumage. As my aunt commented, on an autumn afternoon drenched in light, 'The sun comes over the side. Crystal. Etcetera!' The scene really did sparkle. Protected from the ravages of the global pandemic, with a secure job I could perform remotely, I felt insanely lucky.

Autumn gave way to soggy winter weather. I worked from home; school was suspended. Stupidly, I bought a dog. I cleaned, constantly. I thought about the repetitive labour it takes to maintain a home.

Feminist philosophers Berenice Fisher and Joan Tronto define care as 'everything that we do to maintain, continue and repair our "world" so that we might live in it as well as possible'.[1] In lockdown, the 'world' barely encompassed more than the home. Within it, I experienced daily—even hourly—cycles of entropy and restoration.

The immediate living–learning–working space rapidly decayed, just as every human body and brain eventually does. Grass blew across tiles; dust accreted; someone (who?!) tore a mandarin skin into tiny pieces and piled it neatly next to the compost bin. Mud trudged in. Grubby cat prints. Headphones in knots; a nibbled corn thin discarded on the bath's rim …

I cooked meals for my aunt, which she sometimes gratefully received and sometimes slipped into the freezer. Later, she would hand them to me, saying happily, 'I've got something for you!' In giving, she restored herself to an earlier role in my life.

'An ongoing necessity like dirty dishes needing to be done doesn't produce narrative,' writes poet Ann Boyer. 'It produces quantities, like how many dishes were washed.'[2] I put this book aside. When I resumed work on it, it had become a book about looking after people.

∙∙

What does it take to care for others, in society-wide and more personal terms? How does the Australian welfare state treat those most in need of assistance? What does it involve to look after our kin and kith if—or perhaps when—they unspool?

We were all once vulnerable and will be again. We begin our lives in a condition of dependency as soft, squishy babies and are, we hope, nourished by our caregivers. We deteriorate and become more dependent again: hopefully this happens in old age. Indeed, the pandemic has brought the issue of institutionalised aged care into full public view. Many were confronted with the horrifying realisation that the task of caring for elderly people—our people—has been marketised, falls overwhelming to women and is chronically undervalued.

Who Cares? has a more specific focus than the opening meditation on looking-after-relations might suggest. *Who Cares?* is dedicated to understanding what it is like to live on social security. The looking-after-relation I scrutinise most closely here is between welfare state and person. Collected in this book are stories about life on welfare.

Much public discussion about welfare has understandably been focused on social security payment rates. That $550 supplement lasted three months before being progressively cut back until April 2021.[3] The Morrison government then instituted a new, slightly higher permanent unemployment payment rate.[4]

When lockdowns again dominated the second half of 2021 in many parts of Australia, a patchwork of disaster relief payments substituted for the 2020 raise; these were available only to those who had lost paid work.[5] Food relief services reported unprecedented demand.[6] The Albanese Labor government took office in mid-2022. It declined to commit to increasing JobSeeker in its first budget. As of mid-2022, the JobSeeker rate sits at around $46 per day. The opportunity for life on welfare to change in more meaningful and long-lasting ways has, for now, been refused.

This book is about developments more specific still. I have undertaken research with people affected by two significant welfare measures: the cashless debit card and a pre-employment program called ParentsNext.

Social security recipients compulsorily issued with the controversial cashless debit card from 2016 to 2022 had 80 per cent of their welfare payment quarantined onto a Visa debit card barred from operating at any alcohol or gambling outlet across the nation. The remaining 20 per cent of payments were deposited in the recipient's bank account and could be withdrawn as cash.

ParentsNext is a compulsory pre-employment program for people in receipt of Parenting Payment, either partnered or single, who are looking after pre-school-aged children and who also satisfy a raft of eligibility criteria. ParentsNext mandates participation in an activity each week. Failure to attend or to report attendance online results in payment suspensions.

These are two instructive 'welfare reform' initiatives. Their rationale and effects have much to teach about life on welfare in Australia. While the cashless debit card represents an extreme and ultimately renounced policy experiment, both programs exemplify the increased surveillance of and intervention into poor people's lives, as well as the digitisation and privatisation of welfare delivery.

This book evokes life on welfare as much as it makes arguments about the contemporary welfare state. Others' arguments and my own certainly feature, as I set the experiences I have documented within a larger context. Ultimately, however, argument has a subordinate role to play to evocation. In the chapters to come, I explore the everyday experience of being caught up in these two initiatives, through welfare recipients' own words.

As the opening meditation on my own caring commitments suggests, I hope also to convey that looking after others is an imperative that presses up against my life. 'Welfare recipients' are not these other kinds of people, distant objects of either empathy or distrust, with whom I have nothing in common and from whom I have nothing to learn. The stories collected in this book therefore direct attention to both the uncaring Australian welfare state's failure to look after those seeking support and lived, everyday efforts to sustain life and practise care. Interdependency—our need for and reliance on others—is core to all our lives. This brute fact remains disavowed. Ultimately, these stories urge a change in orientation to the important care that permeates life and which remains unseen and devalued in Australia today.

PART 1
Welfare mutates

1

Look after them?

Valerie stubs her cigarette butts and saves them, leaving them on the front veranda in a tin for a cousin to collect and smoke.

Maude lives alone in her housing trust home, 'just me'. Maude is rarely alone. In the lounge room, lurid fluffy blankets are spread out over a double mattress. 'This is a hospital,' she tells me proudly. 'People come here to heal.'

Natasha volunteers in a not-for-profit mortuary. Relatives come to bathe, tend and clothe their loved one's cool body. Sometimes these family members arrive 'very nervous'. Natasha watches family members slowly relax, reaching to tuck their deceased kin's hair behind ears. Eventually, laughter wafts from the morgue.

∴

This book is about looking after people. Caring for those in need is a role the twentieth-century Australian welfare state promised to fulfil for its citizens. Social security, however, has undergone significant revision since the 1990s, with ever more onerous conditions attached to the receipt of 'income support payments'. Compliance is digitally surveilled, and increased punishments are associated with contravening, or allegedly contravening, those conditions.

By 'income support payments' I refer to the fortnightly government income that citizens and residents in need might qualify for, provided they satisfy certain criteria, including strict means and asset tests: Australia's social security system has 'long been characterised by low and targeted spending'.[1] For instance, Parenting Payment (Single) is the income support payment claimed by sole parents, and the Disability Support Pension is the income support payment claimed by those whose current experience of debility, be it their mental or physical health, prevents them from working. Carer Payment is the payment available to someone who provides near constant care for someone else.

Who Cares? revolves around the lives and perspectives of people affected by two specific welfare measures. I've spent time with people affected by the cashless debit card, which was introduced in the isolated South Australian town of Ceduna in March 2016 and abolished by the Labor government in 2022. In Ceduna, between 2016 and 2022, the cashless debit card—or more simply 'the card'—quarantined 80 per cent of all income support payments received by those aged 65 and under, excluding those on a Veteran Payment or the Age Pension, who could volunteer to be on the card. The quarantined 80 per cent was available on a debit card barred from operating at any alcohol or gambling outlet across Australia. The remaining 20 per cent was deposited into the recipient's personal bank account.

According to the relevant legislation, the trial of the cashless debit card aimed to reduce the amount of social security payments available to be spent on alcohol, gambling and illegal drugs; determine whether such a reduction decreases instances of violence or social harm in trial sites; and encourage 'socially responsible behaviour' more broadly.[2] Those on the card advanced their own analysis. 'I think it is about punishing poor people,' I was told. 'It's about control.'

Valerie, who collects cigarette butts to pass on to a relative who can't afford to buy smokes, is an Aboriginal woman on the Carer Payment who lives in Ceduna; she was never on the card because she is over 65. Many of Valerie's relatives spent time on the card, and she became a vocal critic of it. Maude often has assorted kin and kith in need of a period of rest or recuperation from illness staying with her. She once complained to me that you may as well 'talk to a tree' as ask them to leave. She is also proud of her caring efforts. Maude is an Aboriginal woman who hails from the northern desert region of South Australia but now lives in Ceduna. When I met her, Maude was on an income support payment paid onto the card.

Soon after the first trial commenced in the Ceduna region, a second trial began in the East Kimberley region of Western Australia in April 2016. As of mid-2022, approximately 74 per cent of people on the card in Ceduna were Indigenous, and approximately 83 per cent of people on the card in the East Kimberley were Indigenous.[3] Yet in Ceduna only around 22 per cent of the region's 3500 residents are Indigenous. This stark statistical picture is complicated by the inclusion of the remote Pitjantjatjara community of Yalata in the card trial area. Yalata has approximately 250 residents, but it falls outside of the Ceduna local government area for census purposes.[4] Even accounting for this last fact, the card disproportionately affected Indigenous people in its first two trial sites.

After 2016, the card kept 'spreading', Maude observed to me. The card's expansion beyond Ceduna and the East Kimberley to affect more non-Indigenous people is explained in chapter 3. I will also then outline the developments that led to the origin of the cashless debit card and its demise at the hands of the Albanese government. For now, I insist that the story of the cashless debit card is not just a story about a particular place and the complex situation of remote Aboriginal Australia. Instead, this book is about a particular moment in time, and indeed serves to bookend it. The moment I have documented involved the Australian welfare state intensifying its transition to a more disciplinarian guise, marking an ever-diminishing offer of care to those in need.

So, in order to better understand life on welfare, I turned my attention to another important welfare reform initiative. I have interviewed women across Australia who are in receipt of Parenting Payment, either partnered or single, who are looking after pre-school-aged children and who are compulsory participants in a program called ParentsNext. Natasha, for instance, is a white mother of two teenagers and a toddler and is on Parenting Payment (Single).

ParentsNext was also introduced in 2016 before being rolled out nationally in mid-2018. ParentsNext represents an extension of welfare conditions and digital surveillance to circumstances previously protected from them: parents of babies and infants. Ideal mothers, this program communicates, are 'active' mothers and, ultimately, working mothers.

In a pre-COVID-19 large-scale survey on social class, around 13 per cent of Australians were identified as belonging to a 'precariat'.[5] These are people most affected by poverty and most likely to be wholly or partially dependent on income support payments 'to keep the show on the road', as my interviewee Megan expressed it. For a moment, the crisis conditions of COVID-19 seemed to offer the possibility of a different way of relating to testing circumstances as jobs vanished and swathes of people moved overnight into the maligned category of 'welfare recipient'. Lallie, an African Australian single mum whose analysis of ParentsNext I elaborate in chapter 5, noticed that it was 'very diverse, who was lining up'. It was a 'wake-up call', she thought. Many realised that 'life can happen to people'.

'The COVID supplement that paid welfare recipients a liveable income was the largest anti-poverty measure in Australian history,' writes Ben Eltham.[6] There was nothing inevitable about the political decision to return the JobSeeker rate to a miserly level, where it remains. As wealth and income inequalities deepen in the wake of the pandemic, paying attention to the perspectives of those surviving on welfare seems ever more ethically imperative.

This book insists that we pay attention to the stories told by Valerie, Maude, Natasha, Lallie and many others. The point is not to invite voyeurism, to shock or to horrify the reader but to honour a fundamentally decent impulse: I asked people on welfare about their lives so that I might better understand what it's like to live on welfare. I share here what they shared with me.

··

I embarked on my research into the cashless debit card in mid-2017. More than a decade ago, I had lived with my family in a little coastal locality just outside Ceduna. In 2017, I asked around about who was on the card. An old friend shrugged. 'Everyone's on it,' she said, adding, almost as an afterthought, 'except the ones that have got jobs.'

As of June 2022, around a thousand people in the Ceduna region were on the card. More than half of those on the card were on JobSeeker, around 17 per cent of those on the card were on the Disability Support Pension and almost 20 per cent of those on the card were on a parenting payment.[7]

In Ceduna, I volunteered at a community centre, where mainly Pitjantjatjara-speakers flowed in and out of open doors to have a cup of tea, activate new mobile phones, arrange transport around town and to check the balance of their 'grey card', as the card was locally known. I washed mismatched cups, gave driving lessons and hung around.[8] I went to the local gym, where my instructor cheerfully shared stories of the black snake that had recently slithered under the door and settled under the rowing machine, and I followed the tennis competition, watching matches as galahs cawed and careened overhead. 'Back and forth, back and forth,' my former landlady called out when she spotted me rifling through the crockery in my favourite op shop, which declared proudly on a sign that the cashless debit card could be used through its EFTPOS machine. Between mid-2017 and late 2018 I spent more than three months in Ceduna, coming and going, 'back and forth', from my home in Western Sydney. I made an additional two visits in 2019 and caught up with some of the people I interviewed again in March 2022.

Out on the far west coast of South Australia, an elderly Aboriginal woman took tender care of me. I sometimes rented accommodation near the deep-sea port adjoining Ceduna, where salt is heaped in steep, pristine piles. The nights there were lonely and noisy, as one set of neighbours fought ferociously and another neighbour woke in the early hours to begin his truck driving route. I preferred to 'stop' or 'camp' with Aunty Vera, as it is expressed in Aboriginal English.

I loved driving around with Aunty Vera as she narrated events anchored in place. We went further west to watch a football match, and as we travelled through parched countryside, she evoked a world of rural manual work that has since disappeared. Aboriginal men here formerly worked on state-run railway sidings: her uncles were gangers, heading the railway maintenance gangs. She also held memories of walking down to the old dirt highway and selling rabbits as a child. We passed deserted localities where she'd played in tennis competitions as a teen.

When I interviewed Uncle Bert, he too reminisced about a rich working life after leaving school at 14: station work; painting; bricklaying; driving trucks, tractors and headers; wheat carting—over west. Commercial fishing—up north. Mining, west again. After a health crisis felled him, he found himself unable to work. And as if being looked after by others and not working wasn't degrading enough for Bert, who built a masculine identity around his role as provider, 'along comes the card'.

As a fieldworker, then, I entered into a relation of dependency, constantly asking others for help. Sometimes I borrowed a 4WD: the clutch tended to seize and the whole thing rattled as if it was about to fall apart. 'I'm pretty sure it's registered,' joked my friend, a respected Aboriginal youth worker. Alternatively I borrowed a hair-filled car that another whitefella friend referred to as her 'dog kennel on wheels'. Often, I cadged a bike from an intercultural couple I had got to know; another acquaintance sourced me a helmet as I was warned about the heavy police presence on Ceduna's streets—fines of course apply to riding without a helmet.

I once awoke to get ready for my flight home to find Aunty Vera had filled plastic containers with cold hard-boiled eggs, salad, bread and herbs freshly picked from her garden. She was ironing the clothes I planned to travel in. I continue to correspond with people in Ceduna. I remain, however, a total outsider to this world and would never pretend otherwise.

∴

In 2019 I began interviewing women who were compulsory participants in ParentsNext. These interviewees were all absorbed in a fundamental caregiving activity: they were hard at work looking after, spending their days with and raising babies as young as six months old and/or their small, pre-school-aged children. As of March 2021, around 83 000 parents were participating in ParentsNext; more detailed figures from late 2018 indicate that 95 per cent of participants were then women and 68 per cent of the parents in the program single parents.[9] In chapter 5, I explain how ParentsNext came into being.

I interviewed the energetic advocate Ella Buckland, who was instrumental in stimulating public and media interest in ParentsNext in late 2018.[10] Ella launched a petition, tweeted acerbic commentary about her experiences of the program and started a Facebook page, through which I later recruited a few of my interviewees. As a result of Ella's work, ParentsNext began attracting negative media attention in late 2018. Women revealed that to satisfy the requirement that they participate in an approved activity each week, they felt forced to attend story time sessions at their local library, swimming lessons at their own expense, and playgroups.[11] Later, Ella submitted a Freedom of Information request, which revealed that the then Department of Jobs and Small Business was closely monitoring her activity. 'I couldn't believe what I got,' she told me, about reading the response to her FOI request. 'That they'd been profiling me; that they had media alerts with my name.'

The negative media stories about ParentsNext led to a Senate inquiry, which reported in March 2019.[12] The Senate committee professed concerns about the high rates of payment suspensions incurred by participants in the program, through use of the online Targeted Compliance Framework, which is primarily used to administer an unemployed person's 'mutual obligations'. Natasha, for example, told me the following story.

Natasha's ParentsNext case manager sent her a form to fill out. Originally the form was four pages, double-sided. The case manager scanned and sent her only pages 1 and 3. Natasha's fortnightly payment was halved after Natasha returned the form incomplete, having called and requested the missing pages to no avail. The reduced amount didn't cover her rent, but her landlord was understanding and a friend 'turned up at my place with … you know, she'd gone and got some groceries for me'.

Natasha's experience of having her income abruptly stopped is not an isolated incident. Between ParentsNext's national rollout in mid-2018 and August 2021, more than '55 000 parents received 159 000 suspensions lasting an average of five days on each occasion'.[13] According to journalist Luke Henriques-Gomes's forensic analysis of this suspension regime, 85 per cent of parents on ParentsNext who had their income support temporarily cut off in the 2018–19 financial year were found not to have been at fault.¹⁴ This was the case for Natasha, whose full payment was quickly reinstated, after having to depend on a friend to feed her children over the weekend.

From late 2019 to 2021 I talked in depth to around twenty women like Natasha, who were mandated to participate in ParentsNext. I circulated a call-out for interviewees on social media. Women living across Australia reached out, wanting to talk, despite a professed anxiety among some about contacting a university researcher to speak about a program that they were required to participate in, in order to keep receiving income. As my interviewee Eloise put it, 'they hold the power over me feeding my kid'. I met up with women living in Sydney and regional New South Wales but also spoke with some interviewees over the phone if they lived too far away, because of COVID-19 lockdowns, or because they were consumed by the utterly unpredictable task of wrangling small children, a predicament familiar to me.

∴

The first scenario involves introducing the reader to people whose lives might well seem radically different. Remote-living First Nations people are frequently represented as enduring the most abject conditions imaginable within this wealthy settler colonial nation.¹⁵ Many of those people I got to know in Ceduna were extremely impoverished—they came into the community centre to use the computers because, rather obviously, they didn't own one. One morning, an inmate put through a call to the centre's office from Port Augusta prison, knowing he would reach numerous kin and friends to talk to. Incarceration is an utterly ordinary circumstance in this world. On another occasion, a highly respected elderly woman I had encountered months ago told me she still had my phone number written down and recently thought about calling it to relay that she had 'no food'. However, she continued, 'No credit.'

In more positive terms, I spent time with multilingual First Nations people closely tied to their ancestral country. I worked with one such Pitjantjatjara woman, Elsie Numitja Illi, to record her stories and publish a 'little book' about her life. Elsie has a keen sense of the significance of her life and the interest it potentially holds for others.

In beginning her story, Elsie describes being born out on the Nullarbor Plain. There were 'no doctors, no nurses'. Elsie's mum laboured 'under a tree', with her female kin present.[16] As the corpus of anthropological writing about Aboriginal traditions attests, birth 'is a moment of extreme power'. The 'process of giving birth and the remaining placenta are things from which men must be guarded'.[17]

What happened next is also of crucial relevance. 'As with all bush babies, the government gave me a choice of birthdays,' explains Elsie. Offered 1 January or 1 July, the family specified the mid-year date. However, 'they gave me first of January, 1954'.[18] That pattern—the state exercising excessive and, in this case, arbitrary control about intimate matters—resonates with Aboriginal critiques of the card and has been a constant in Elsie's life.

Who Cares? certainly documents lives shaped by colonial contact, dispossession and loss, as well as prison stints, insecure housing, addiction, long-term unemployment, ill health and the like. However, it also revolves around the stories of people who are probably more likely to strike readers as familiar. I spoke with women whose middle-class trajectories were interrupted by a conjunction of unexpected events beyond their control. Some of my interviewees had come to depend temporarily on the welfare state, much to their surprise.

Ella, for instance, told me about the week things fell apart. She was sick and struggling to look after her baby daughter, who was then around six or seven months old. She went to her mum's place in regional New South Wales, 'my bags packed for two weeks'. She continued, 'And then he dumped us via email.' Ella found herself stranded away from her doctor, whose continuity of care she greatly valued, and far from her former life as an educated professional. Lying on a bed, her daughter's cot beside her, she gazed at glow-in-the-dark stickers she'd plastered to the ceiling as a little girl. 'Wow! Definitely made it,' she commented wryly.

Natasha's background was more solidly working class. Since leaving school at the age of 15 she has held a wide range of administrative and sales roles. When I met her, she was on Parenting Payment (Single), recovering from a broken wrist and looking after her three-year-old and two teenage kids. Natasha explained to me that her ParentsNext case manager required her to undertake an 'approved activity' each week, which might include volunteering. And Natasha had become involved at the not-for-profit mortuary some time ago, as sketched in this chapter's opening scene. She immediately found it a powerful experience that wove life threads together. Having her own losses, Natasha also volunteers with another support group. But it's her work at the mortuary that we talked of at length. 'It might seem weird to say that I love my job and I enjoy it,' she mused, 'but I really do.'

Birth and death: 'there are a lot more similarities than people might think', observed Natasha. 'Death is labour, just like birth,' writes Rachel Buchanan. 'Both events resist schedules.'[19] Perhaps both are also best thought of as processes that involve disintegration, I found myself contemplating after spending an intensely philosophical two hours talking with Natasha in a club in a regional New South Wales town, poker machines whirring, spinning and dinging in the background.

Natasha next told me that her ParentsNext case manager approved of her volunteering but sought to rearrange and standardise the hours she was devoting to it, which were carefully organised around her children and the schedules of two involved dads. ParentsNext also involved monitoring Natasha's volunteering through a reporting app. Compliance and threat entered her commitments. Working alongside grieving families and impassioned volunteers, Natasha commented, 'I didn't want them to think I was doing my volunteering work just to satisfy my ParentsNext requirements.'

∙∙

In the early twentieth century the Australian welfare state began to take shape with the advent of pension payments, which were envisaged as an exchange for a lifetime of work. As the twentieth century approached its end, this same welfare state underwent systematic reform. In fact, since the 1990s, the Australian welfare state has been subject to a series of evolving, continuous reforms.[20]

More conditional and punitive welfare regimes, which seek to encourage entrepreneurial forms of responsibility and to keep unemployed persons busy, have been identified as a characteristic of neoliberal societies across the Global North.[21] In more everyday terms, increasingly onerous conditions are now attached to the receipt of social security payments. These heightened conditions range from reporting requirements to the kinds of time and commitments expected of people in return for receiving social security payments.

Since 2007 Australia has taken 'conditionality' even further, placing limitations on what some people can spend their welfare moneys on through the introduction of 'income management' tools such as the BasicsCard and the cashless debit card. As well as becoming more conditional, the Australian welfare state has also become more punitive over these same decades: payment suspensions are incurred if recipients contravene these proliferating conditions. In sum, 'sanctions', or 'penalties that reduce or terminate benefits in response to client noncompliance', can be understood as 'the ultimate expression of welfare's disciplinary turn'.[22]

Welfare has also gone digital in the same period, across numerous countries. In South Africa and parts of India, for example, social assistance is secured only after the highly controversial and intrusive collection of biometric data—such as an iris scan or fingerprints. In many places, eligibility assessment is automated, such as within the UK's Universal Credit system. Critics point out that a lack of internet access and/or an applicant's digital skills serve as barriers to applicants accessing their full entitlements through Universal Credit and other systems. Australia's retrospective Robodebt program made clear the large volume of errors that might result from the digital welfare state's 'rigidity' and 'robotic application of rules', a common feature of automated systems that also leads to increased sanctions.[23]

As I write, Australia has just embarked on a new phase of digital transformation. From July 2022, some employment services are be provided online through chat bots and machine-learning platforms designed to 'assist jobseekers in self-managing their own return from welfare-to-work'. Named 'Workforce Australia', face-to-face services are to be retained for 'those jobseekers considered harder-to-help'.[24] A new and exacting points system will monitor compliance to the conditions attached to social security receipt.

Further, these 'neoliberal welfare states', as Australia can now be termed, are also thoroughly marketised.²⁵ In effect, the post-1990s welfare state is a disaggregated system: many of its core functions have been devolved to a constellation of private interests that generate profits through the provision of services conceived of as a suite of products. The term 'welfare state', digital or otherwise, implies a monolithic, hefty, coherent thing. Given the fragmentation that privatisation has entailed, I rely on the readily recognised notion of a 'welfare state' with some reservations, referring sometimes instead to a welfare 'system'.

More specifically, the contract to issue and administer the privatised cashless debit cards was awarded to a financial product company, Indue. From 2016 to March 2022, the contract with Indue cost the federal government $60 390 692, a figure that excludes the original cost to 'build' the system, which came to $2 870 675.²⁶ In Ceduna, the cashless debit card or 'grey card' was also referred to as the 'Indue card', and the Indue helpline number was prominently displayed in the community centre where I spent time. 'They have taken all the poor people and sold them to a private company!' one woman on the card told me, early on in my research.

The profits generated through ParentsNext are more dispersed. One of my interviewees explained to me that after being initially contacted via the federal social security agency, Centrelink, to have one's eligibility assessed, it continues to feel like ParentsNext has something to do with Centrelink: 'But you ring Centrelink and they [say] "we don't deal with it". "But I'm still receiving my money from you."' It's then my interviewee realised, 'They've sold you to the Department of Jobs, who've sold you to the provider.' The 1970s US-based Welfare Rights movement lost momentum, anthropologist Maggie Dickinson argues, through this very process: it's not clear which entity to direct one's demands towards.²⁷

ParentsNext is therefore a program delivered by a range of for-profit 'providers', many of which are also contracted to provide services to the unemployed. Alternatively, they might be non government or community organisations, involved in more general service provision and even social justice advocacy, such as the Brotherhood of St Laurence. These providers collect $600 every six months for each participant they administer as part of the program—a significant disincentive for exempting women where there is some ambiguity about their eligibility, which was the case for Ella.[28]

∴

Many researchers have examined the historical context for and ideas animating these reform processes, as well as unemployed, disabled and sole parents' experiences of them.[29] What do I add to the conversation?

Writing on welfare is generally the preserve of social policy analysts, who privilege quantitative methods. Words like 'disadvantage' and 'barriers' are frequently used, and sometimes I need them too. But there is no denying that social science verbiage and statistics serve to abstract circumstances that are messy, particular, contradictory and complicated, as all human circumstances are. *Who Cares?* offers instead an up-close, humane and grounded ethnographic account of life on welfare. I have sought to draw nearer to the people caught up in this endlessly reforming welfare system, foregrounding their perspectives, analyses and experiences.

Second, committing to this more holistic approach directed my attention to welfare recipients' manifold efforts in the world, as I documented lives unfolding beyond and outside people's interactions with welfare. In other words, there's much *more* to Valerie, Maude and Natasha's lives than being 'welfare recipients', a category that defines people exclusively by their relationship to paid work. This book explores that *more*.[30] My interviewees' ties to the people with whom their lives are enmeshed, as well as their dreams, schemes, desires, love stories and theories about the world, all feature within these pages.

Further, I document here the burdensome displacement of care responsibilities onto people whose circumstances are already worn. To state that poor people look after their own is hackneyed, I know. Instead, I seek to acknowledge that looking after people is hard. Caring for others emerges as one of the many kinds of labour that people receiving social security engage in, among other everyday efforts 'to keep life going'.[31] I am thinking here of Maude's mix of acceptance, exasperation and exhaustion as she works to maintain her household. As American anthropologist Catherine Fennell argues, where the rollback of welfare provision compels people to 'lean on themselves and proximate others, like friends and kin, to guarantee basic care', those in a position to provide such care step 'toward their obligations with a mix of pleasure and trepidation'.[32] In less extreme circumstances, too, taking care of others is necessary work that is constantly going on; many of the welfare recipients I interviewed routinely engage in it. Welfare discourse, I came to see, obscures the constancy and centrality of care to all our lives.

∴

My anthropology students read a poem titled 'ologist' by Alison Whittaker from the collection *Blakwork*. Whittaker writes:

> bury them
> astride the savage, noble and the vital, and
> while you're at it
> bury me in there with all them rioters.
>
> discover nothing.[33]

I read the one-line stanza as a command: discover nothing. This represents a powerful rejection of an intrusive colonial gaze, which coolly dissects First Nations peoples as objects of interest and inquiry. The potential of anthropology to represent unwelcome scrutiny, in the very same moment as the welfare system ramps up its monitoring, was an ever-present tension in my research, informing a degree of holding back and an acute awareness of when and why others withheld from me.[34]

Yet I still embrace anthropology, which demands an effort to get close to life as it is experienced by others. I focus on people's lives not because within individuals lies the source and remedy of their poverty but because the individual person 'is the site where life is lived, meanings are made, will is exercised … determinations take effect'.[35] I've said that there's much more to Maude, Vera and Natasha's lives than their categorisation as welfare recipients: anthropology directs us to this excess. Importantly, then, anthropology ideally involves a 'painful porosity' or openness to others, whose objectives, insights, categories, experiences and feelings serve to affect, teach and change both the research and the researcher.[36]

In more concrete terms, anthropology deals with the everyday and ponders seemingly insignificant, easily skipped-over details. Take Valerie's tin of collected cigarette butts. What might I make of this habit of hers? Cigarettes are simultaneously a medium of exchange, providing Valerie with the opportunity for generosity despite her limited material means, and a poisonous killer. Since the early 1980s, the Australian state has prioritised the health of its citizens over the profits of the tobacco industry; state efforts have drastically reduced smoking rates over the last few decades.[37] For this reason, cigarettes are subject to heavy consumption taxes.

It was savvy, smoking research participants, both those on the card and single mums on ParentsNext, who wryly pointed out to me that they are 'taxpayers'. They understood the power of a moral opposition between 'bludger' and taxpayer in debates about social security spending. In fact, Australia moves ever further away from a progressive income tax system and towards a system that raises revenue through measures we might usefully think of as 'flat taxes', such as consumption taxes, road tolls and fines.[38] These burden poorer people disproportionately. The line between welfare recipient and taxpayer may be morally charged, but in reality it is not easily drawn and should be perceived as a political rather than empirical formulation.

Further, smoking is gratifying, as well as addictive and ruinous to one's health. The anthropologist Megan Warin describes the way sugary fast foods and smoking may well imperil uncertain futures but are a source of immediate pleasure in the present, holding difficult realities in abeyance.[39] All of this—history, context, policy, cravings, pleasure, everyday practice— was in the mix, as Valerie carefully set aside that cigarette end, stashing it in an empty packet before we continued our walk up the main street together. Ultimately, Valerie paused to hold another's desires in mind in this moment. When her cousin passed by to collect those crumpled ends, he would have known that.

∵

I have already listed some of the tangible and essential things people handed over to me: their spare bed, a bike helmet. However, anthropologists' dependency on their hosts is a deeper matter still. People entrusted their stories, fears and perspectives to me, some urging me to pass their opinions 'back', 'write a submission to cancel it' or 'put it through' to 'the government'; others hoping that I would help 'get the story out there' to a wider public. This role comes with significant responsibilities: how to be an ethical witness, to get these lives down on the page, without exploiting them?

I seek here to write about life on welfare with immediacy, attempting to capture life's very liveliness. Maria Tumarkin writes effectively of tough lives lived out 'on a highway where they are repeatedly hit by passing trucks'. Tumarkin continues, 'As they are bandaging their wounds, cleaning them out with rainwater, putting bones back into sockets, another truck's oncoming … Most people have a truck going over them at some period of their life. But on a highway you don't get one or two. You get a convoy. They don't stop. That's the point. The recurrence is the point.'[40]

Perhaps this metaphor captured me because I thought of a mate's dad, killed by a truck as he walked home along a poorly lit, often-trod road on the scrubby outskirts of Ceduna. I also admire and hope to share in Tumarkin's search for a way to enliven the writing about difficult lives, avoiding abstraction.

This book includes people's voices when they narrate, opine and analyse, when they share with great poignancy but also when they swear, joke, mangle grammar, elaborate fanciful theories and half finish a thought. I am deeply bonded to some of the people who appear pseudonymously in this book. I also interviewed racists, evangelists, sleazes and untrustworthy souls. I am not willing to suggest that a condition of entitlement to social assistance and care is goodness and make judicious use of confronting material. Jaggedness is a quality of lives subject to constant disruptions, both dramatic and quotidian; I encountered a jumpiness in many of my interlocutors, some of whom almost twitched with 'stress', as one Ceduna interviewee emphasised on the numerous occasions I recorded his stories.

If life events are hurled at them rather than them exerting control over their circumstances, I came to understand that both the card and ParentsNext often represented one more such interruption—a decision about daily life circumstances over which people hold no control and which in turn takes away more control.

∴

Chapters 2 and 3, 'Sustenance' and 'Surveillance', narrate a brief history of welfare in Australia. Chapter 4 is titled 'Stressed out to be on the card' and evokes life on the cashless debit card. In chapter 5, 'Why are you crying? We're here to help you', I turn my attention to ParentsNext. Chapter 6, 'They think we're rubbish', discusses the card and ParentsNext together as I explore more deeply the shame associated with welfare. Finally, in chapter 7, I close by homing in on the important work of caring for others in 'Had to be done'. This closing chapter also involves an exploration of the meaning and potential of dependency.

The title of this opening chapter, 'Look after them?', comes from a conversation with Maude. I called Maude one wet winter evening from a busy inner Sydney railway station to express my 'sorry'—sorrow—after a significant Aboriginal figure had died. Maude told me she had been at home crying for her relative; she said our conversation lifted her 'spirit up'. We agreed he had lived a full life, busily involved in community and cultural activity right to the end. And after all, he was 'old'—in his sixties.

Our conversation turned to another recent death. Rain hammered down, bodies pressed past and I found myself unable to follow the details. I became really sad, thinking about these losses and feeling very far away. It was then I sensed our conversation shift: my sympathy was of no comfort to Maude. She reminded me, firmly: 'This is how we live out here. In the sticks. Look after them.'

Maude—that central pillar in a large Pitjantjatjara household that breathes in, filling up and expanding, then exhales, releasing, shrinking. There was always a lot going on in that home: storytelling, sickness, state intervention and the swapping of 'grey cards'; incarceration, debt, fighting, healing; marathon NITV-watching efforts, political analysis, mugs of tea on the veranda ... Maude's comment was enigmatic but stimulating too.

Maude articulates a fundamental orientation to people rather than productivity, the profoundly asocial value that often drives me.[41] I've learnt much about what really matters through knowing Maude and others. I make this claim cautiously. I have undertaken research with people deemed in need of intervention, reform and even rescue. How could I bear to foreground the practice of care given the situation in Ceduna, where high rates of family violence, premature death and sickness are very real? I am not trying to deny these aspects of life but to see and understand people's caring efforts in this place.

An argument for the value of caregiving is easier to advance in the case of ParentsNext. I might build on a cultural script about the importance of primary carers spending time with children in the early years and intermittent public ambivalence about the institutionalisation of early childhood through the use of long day care. Here I run the risk of sanctifying the maternal role. My interviewees' frank admissions about the shadowy dimensions of parenthood guard against this.

Ultimately, I think Maude sought to underline a powerful principle, which accepts dependency, vulnerability and interconnectedness as inescapable realities. As anthropologist David Graeber noted shortly before his death, COVID-19 jolted us into confronting 'the actual reality of human life'. As if waking from a dream, he thought, it was now clear 'that we are a collection of fragile beings taking care of one another'. Further, 'those who do the lion's share of this care work that keeps us alive'—in a paid capacity—'are overtaxed, underpaid and daily humiliated'. I would add that many who do the everyday work to keep others going are themselves cast as 'welfare dependent'. Their efforts in the world and, indeed, their full humanity is often not seen. Graeber's plea was that in a post–COVID-19 world, we hang on to that reality rather than falling 'back to sleep'.[42] Maude puts it more simply in stating, 'This is how we live.'

'Look after them' is a fact, but I also hear it as an exhortation.

2

Sustenance

Robby was on the cashless debit card when I first met him. He would have the story begin like this: 'But the government, the white man, Captain Cook, come and said, "No."'

What did he mean by 'no'?

'Captain Cook lied,' Robby said. 'When he come over and he looked around to see if there was any activity … he went back and said, "No, there's nothing. There's nothing here."' Robby concluded, 'Someone back in England lied, "There's nobody occupying the land."'

No activity. No occupation recognised as legitimate, sovereign occupation. So, in January 1788, eleven tall ships sailed into Cadigal people's waters. Along the coves and slender fingers of the pre-colonial Sydney Basin, clanswomen fished from bark canoes that served as 'mobile kitchens'. They fished with shellfish hooks called burra and line, 'cooking on small fires atop clay pads on the canoe floor and breastfeeding children as they went'.[1] On these still waters, then, life-sustaining activities were undertaken together. Women fished as they fed infants and were fishing to feed others. The effort expended in catching and cooking fish was not distinct, categorised as work and pursued separate from the nurturance of children.

Then, on those shores, on the basis of 'lies', unloaded the impoverished riffraff of Georgian English society in the midst of the upheavals set in train by industrial capitalism. In England at this time, the regulated rhythms of long working days were emerging as factories opened up; waves of rural to urban migration gathered pace; cottage diets were replaced with the substandard fare that became, first, the colonial diet and then Aboriginal people's rations: white flour and sweet tea.²

Crimes of poverty were heavily penalised, creating the conditions for the New South Wales colony's founding. In Georgian England, poor laws dating from the Elizabethan era provided for those in need if their families could not support them. Just before Queen Victoria's ascension to the throne, the New Poor Law of 1834 sought to limit the amount of 'outdoor relief' being claimed by 'paupers' in need of assistance; that is, unconditional financial support paid to supplement inadequate earnings. After the numbers seeking such relief had swelled at the end of the Napoleonic Wars, the workhouse test was introduced. This resulted in a radical reduction of the relief rolls as well as the founding of grim institutions devoted to moral and behavioural reform.³ Workhouses were 'places for punishment', which served to 'scare people on the outside and to produce docility on the inside'.⁴

In a strictly legal sense, poor laws were not imported into the Australian colonies. Non-Aboriginal people who found themselves destitute in Australian colonies did not derive a right to assistance from their place of residence. Instead, they approached seemingly private charitable organisations that possessed discretionary power—although these church and civil society outfits were generally in receipt of substantial government funds.⁵ Arguments against introducing poor laws in Australia were made from different perspectives. On the one hand, an argument was made against a system that forced a tier of the state, at the level of the local parish, to assume responsibility for those in need. This, disapproving conservative voices expressed, only encouraged dependency and dissuaded manly self-reliance. The labour movement of the time also valorised the goal of self-reliance. The labour movement therefore also opposed poor laws but for a different reason, indignantly highlighting the cruel and dehumanising aspects of the 1834 law, which was reviled and feared by the English working class.⁶

The absence of a poor law system in the Australian colonies did not mean an absence of poverty. A series of charitable institutions 'for various problematic elements of the white population' was established in Sydney in the early decades of the nineteenth century.[7] Originally envisaged to alleviate distress, these institutions quickly moved towards a more corrective role, aimed at fostering industrious habits in those interned and at removing their contaminating influence from society. Because poor whites were mostly ex-convicts, they were regarded as especially depraved.

Shortly after one of these charitable institutions, the Benevolent Society of New South Wales, opened in 1813, Governor Macquarie founded the Native Institution at Parramatta in 1814 putatively to administer aid to Aboriginal people, especially in the wake of accelerating dispossession as settler colonial rural industries expanded.[8] This institution was intended to prevent Aboriginal children's contact with the 'corrupting' influence of the colony's poor whites. While these two 'problem' populations were to be kept apart, in practical terms they were treated in similar ways: subject to supervision, restraint and long workdays. Poor laws might not have travelled to the Australian colonies, but the crucial distinction between the undeserving and deserving poor certainly took root and was applied in the nineteenth century to both impoverished whites and Aboriginal people. It is important also to emphasise differences in their treatment: at the Native Institution an experiment was being conducted as to whether Aboriginal children were 'teachable'.[9] This institution was short-lived for numerous reasons, including the fact that Aboriginal parents quickly realised and objected to the fact that young girls were being trained for domestic servitude.[10]

Macquarie, my workplace's namesake, distributed blankets to Aboriginal people as an act of charity; founded an ostensibly benevolent but deeply corrective institution; and went on to order armed forces to shoot Aboriginal people involved in resisting pastoral expansion on the Cumberland Plain south-west of Sydney. The 1816 Appin massacre resulted in the deaths of at least fourteen Aboriginal people. Macquarie ordered his troops to display the bodies of slain men prominently in order to strike fear into the hearts of their surviving kin and clans-people. Two deceased men were hung from trees, and Cannabaygal's skull was sent to England.[11] Here reigned a gruesome 'frontier culture of terror'.[12]

New Poor Law thinking certainly influenced the way Aboriginal people were treated on and off missions in the nineteenth century, via the preferential supply of blankets and rations to the morally deserving and to encourage work.[13] Their poverty, however, was both produced by and experienced within a crucible of extreme and overt violence.

∴

This patchwork of charities, with strong moral overtures and discretionary powers, persisted into the twentieth century, which witnessed the emergence of new ideas. At the turn of the century, as is well known, the federated nation of Australia came into being—envisaged as a white working-man's paradise. What became known as the White Australia Policy excluded and expelled non-whites, who represented the threat of cheap labour.

Inside this newly created fortress, Aboriginal people were at first believed to be fated for extinction. Aboriginal people were subject to repressive state protectionist acts, formulated around the late nineteenth century and into the first decades of the twentieth. While the year and detail of these state-based protection regimes varied, they each enacted a separate legal category for Aboriginal people, whose lives were closely controlled. These legislative acts instituted a welfare system distinct from the welfare state; appointed 'protectors' nominally had Aboriginal 'welfare' as their concern.[14]

The question of old age pensions was being heavily debated in Australia around this time, as it was in Britain, New Zealand and Denmark. Pension proponents sought and were ultimately able to 'leave behind much of the moral and ideological vocabulary of pauperism' endemic to Poor Law thinking.[15] In 1900, old age pensions were first legislated for in Victoria and then in New South Wales. In 1908, a federal act modelled on the New South Wales one provided for old age and invalid pensions, which were means-tested. It was within the pension debates that welfare as a right was asserted. It was framed as a reward for the service of waged work already given to the white nation.

Other voices argued for a system more akin to charity, available only to the morally upright. 'All the pension acts had restrictions based on racial exclusions, length of residency, spouse desertion, income and criminal convictions,' clarifies historian John Murphy. Further, most included 'vaguely defined tests of character, particularly sobriety'.[16] Still, the federal pension scheme entailed a significant shift.

What did this shift mean for poor white women? Patricia Harris evokes the private and personal 'nature of philanthropy', which meant 'women of different class backgrounds came face-to-face with each other in the process of judgment and relief'. Over the course of the first half of the twentieth century this 'was gradually transformed to the impersonal, bureaucratic methods of provision with which we are familiar today'.[17] Indeed, despite the presence of gendered imagery throughout the pension debate, as manly independence was invoked, white women made up the majority of applicants for the New South Wales pension scheme. Significantly, the old age pension schemes 'treated single men and women as equal citizens in their own right'.[18]

Explicit provisions in the pension acts made Aboriginal people ineligible, as well as various other non-white peoples. For example, 'Asiatics' were also explicitly excluded from claiming the New South Wales pension, which in practical terms affected an established and substantial Chinese community 'and advertised that no more were welcome as migrants'.[19] In the case of First Nations people, they 'were being told their dispossession was complete and they had no place in an imagining of the national community'.[20]

In this same period came the landmark Harvester judgment of 1907, which set the first minimum wage standard. While it took more than a decade for the payment of living wages to take effect, this decision illustrates the enmeshment of ideals of manhood, nationhood, whiteness and dignity. A nuclear family structure was normalised as Judge Higgins assumed a wage-earning head of the household, a woman whose responsibility it was to maintain family life and the home and two or three children who should all be entitled to live 'in frugal comfort'.[21]

Keeping non-white labour out protected the possibility of high wages within the antipodean social laboratory. Wages were to be the 'frontline weapon against poverty', rendering state assistance a kind of 'secondary safety-net'.[22] This model has been termed the 'wage earners' welfare state' and helps explain why Australian welfare payments have long been so residual and receipt of them highly stigmatised.[23] The centrality of white male waged work to this account also explains why historically 'women predominated amongst the poor, overwhelmingly because of the absence or failure of a male breadwinner'.[24]

••

In the 1930s, a deep Depression engulfed the capitalist world. Novelist Ruth Park, who fictionalised poor inner-city lives, depicted the scenes surrounding the Sydney Harbour Bridge's assembly: while the 'monstrous hump' was crawling with men, everywhere more stood knotted 'on corners, in doorways', out of work.[25] Their poverty was public and acute.

Throughout the Depression, unemployed men were eligible for a combination of sustenance and relief work. The conditions attached to the provision of support varied between the Australian states and comprised a combination of vouchers and cash payments: 'the dole' or 'susso' (meaning sustenance) in vernacular terms. In the main, applicants 'had to be without work for a prescribed length of time' and show that 'they had substantially exhausted their income and resources'.[26]

Relief work, which involved being paid to do labouring work at rates 'marginally better than the dole', was also a feature of this period: relief work was intended to prevent 'idleness' and 'dispersed men around the country'.[27] Relief projects primarily entailed constructing sewage and water supply systems and building roads and bridges, but also included reclaiming swamplands, installing bowling greens and beautifying public gardens. 'Rural development' was also considered a priority, partly because 'authorities thought it was prudent to remove potentially restive unemployed men from the radicalising influence of the city'.[28] Relief was again conceptualised in this period as the alleviation of pain or distress, in order to ensure that indigent families had enough to eat. Despite the watershed passing of the pension acts, then, Depression relief can be understood as a legacy of the new poor laws in its moral-behavioural considerations and delivery of emergency support only in desperate circumstances.[29]

Nonetheless, the movement towards less charitable and more bureaucratic models of assistance, which had begun in the wake of the 1890s Depression and which resulted in the pension, further ensued as the twentieth century progressed. Throughout the 1930s, Australian politicians drew heavily on the British experience to propose a contributory social insurance scheme, a plan that was slowly abandoned.[30] The model adopted instead remains unaltered: welfare spending in Australia is funded from general taxpayer revenue, which means that receipt of social security payments is stringently means- and asset-tested.

Moral-behavioural concerns became increasingly 'muted' from the 1940s onwards.[31] This period witnessed a series of significant initiatives. In 1941 the Menzies government instituted 'child endowment' payments paid at a flat rate for second and subsequent children.[32] Then, from late 1941 to 1949, the Labor Party experienced nearly a decade in power. Haunted by the Depression, unemployment itself rather than unemployed individuals became the problem and the 'object of governance'.[33] The *Unemployment and Sickness Benefits Act of 1944* provided for cash benefits 'by statute rather than discretion'.[34] The post-war period was characterised by full employment, a general level of affluence and pockets of hidden poverty. In sum: 'At the very moment that the Australian welfare state emerged it was relegated to a residual role.'[35]

∙∙

The twentieth century witnessed growing public and government awareness about the rising population of Aboriginal people who had survived the onslaught of invasion, many of whom were of mixed descent. Emphasis shifted towards assimilation, which imagined a future of full citizenship for people whose Aboriginality had ceased to become a source of identity or difference.[36] In chapter 1, I stated that looking after those in need is a role the twentieth-century Australian welfare state promised to fulfil for its citizens. I used the word deliberately: this was a category that excluded Aboriginal people throughout most of the twentieth century.[37]

Explicit provisions disqualified Aboriginal people from income support payments, industrial awards and the electoral franchise until the 1940s. However, one mechanism for realising Aboriginal assimilation 'was the granting of exemptions' to Aboriginal individuals 'from the special bodies of State and Territory law'.[38] And, following various amendments, Aboriginal people might, in theory, be eligible for select provisions of the welfare state if they had been so exempted or excluded from the legal category of Aboriginal or if their 'character, standard of intelligence and social development' made it 'reasonable' to grant eligibility.[39] Hence, Murphy characterises Aboriginal relations to the twentieth-century welfare state as a complex question of 'conditional inclusion' rather than exclusion. As assimilationist thinking developed throughout the twentieth century, the criteria for eligibility for some social security payments became increasingly based on behaviour and 'civilised' norms.[40]

For example, many Aboriginal mothers were entitled to claim child endowment payments after the Menzies government introduced them in 1941. Aboriginal eligibility, historian Ann McGrath notes, was 'highly conditional' on the applicant's 'lifestyle', especially housing. 'If they were nomadic or sustained themselves by hunting and gathering, they were ineligible.'[41] McGrath explains: 'Missions were entitled to collect such endowments on behalf of the children under 16 if they fully fed, clothed, housed and maintained them.'[42] While child endowment payments advanced white women's rights, Aboriginal mothers' caregiving role was undermined on missions, which in effect claimed that Aboriginal children were the dependants of the missionary institution.

When I interviewed Bert, introduced briefly in chapter 1, he talked of his own varied working life and of the work available to his father and uncles as he was growing up in the 1950s. 'So there was plenty of work around,' he began. 'And, yeah that's why all my family and everyone, Nungas [South Australian Aboriginal people] were all scattered along the railway line.' They were 'needed' Bert stated simply, 'for wheat lumping, for shearing'. The 'old days' were 'really good' for Aboriginal people, Bert mused. He also told me, 'You know, we were dependent on child endowment.' Bert's father, like a lot of Aboriginal men in the district, left the mission and moved around looking for work. '[T]he family was left behind, to fend, and the husbands went away.'

'Left behind' with his mother and siblings and subsisting on social security, Bert's childhood days were in fact filled with hunting, which he fondly recalled. Bert's recollections complicate McGrath's point: his family proudly maintained a way of life that mixed traditional, skilful methods of food provisioning with wage labour and consumer goods. He tells stories of hardship but of freedom, too.

As had been the case with child endowment payments since 1941, protectors secured Aboriginal eligibility to social security payments in 1959, except in cases where they were 'nomadic or primitive'.[43] However, provisions entitled these social security payments to be made to third parties on behalf of eligible applicants and authorities. That meant protectors and reserve and station managers secured the bulk of these newly available payments, passing only a token portion to individuals. It was not just Aboriginal wages that were stolen then, as has now been well established, but also their social security entitlements. In fact, on marginal pastoral stations across northern Western Australia, profitability in the midst of changing global economic conditions was ensured by the combination of low rents, exploited Aboriginal labour and the misappropriation of old age pension cheques to which Aboriginal people camped on the stations were entitled from 1960 onward. This practice was widespread until around 1966, when it started to become more difficult.[44]

In 1966 the 'final caveat' regarding 'nomadic or primitive' Aboriginal applicants was removed.[45] From here on in Aboriginal people were fully included in the social security system in a statutory sense—but in practical terms often continued to be excluded. Pressure to ensure that Aboriginal people were receiving the social security payments they were entitled to as individuals grew throughout the 1960s, and the era of equal entitlement on equal terms began in the 1970s. It was to prove short-lived, as chapter 3 details.

∴

Pension acts conceived of those welfare payments as earned in old age by those who had served the nation through work but explicitly excluded Aboriginal people. Yet Aboriginal and Torres Strait Islander people were centrally involved in many early settler colonial economies. Perhaps most famous is the situation in the northern pastoral industry, which remained dependent on exploited stock workers and domestic servants, as well as claiming Aboriginal people's social security entitlements, into the 1960s. There are many other examples. It is worth hearing a range of stories from across the continent and beyond it to appreciate the diversity of this long-erased activity.

On the south coast of New South Wales, Yuin families used their intimate knowledge of local environs to strip and sell wattle bark used in tanneries from the early period of first contact in the 1820s. When the size of landholdings increased in the late nineteenth century, a period of rapid dispossession ensued. Increasingly confined to the Wallaga Lake reserve, from the 1930s to the 1970s Aboriginal people on the south coast engaged in bean- and pea-picking. This work involved heavy manual labour with poor working conditions, but oral histories reveal that it was a desirable alternative for Yuin people: picking enabled families to work together.[46]

There is an echo here of those scenes of Cadigal women's fishing and breastfeeding early on in this chapter. Although some Yuin men held continuous employment in local sawmills while women and children picked, often whole families worked in parallel. This was a way of labouring in keeping with pre-contact life, whereby hunting and food collecting was a social and collaborative activity undertaken with kin. Indeed, it remains so. The social dimensions of plucking bush medicine and cooking kangaroo tails on hot coals—malu wipu—were often highlighted to me when I was in Ceduna and out bush. These tasks were always shared and involved gathering people together to accomplish them, regardless of how many hands were needed for the task.

Far away from Yuin Country, in Torres Strait, young men began engaging in waged work in the latter half of the nineteenth century, retiring to work in their own gardens as they aged. Rigid racial hierarchies structured a diverse labour force, which supplied pearl shell for buttons.

Malays, Japanese and Pacific Islanders were paid more than Torres Strait Islander men, and Aboriginal people and Papuans were paid less. The post-war period saw both increased agitation for equal wages and the collapse of the maritime industry. In the 1960s, Queensland relaxed its control of Torres Strait Islander movement, and Torres Strait Islander gangs worked in the hot interior, building new infrastructure across Queensland, the Northern Territory and Western Australia.[47]

Pitjantjatjara- and Yankunytjatjara-speakers sold dingo scalps from around the 1920s onwards, among them probably the ancestors of those people who mill about in Ceduna's community centre. Anangu (a word meaning both person and people) traded with 'doggers', who exchanged the scalps for tea, sugar and flour, then sold them for cash to government agents, or they travelled to places where they were paid directly in cash. That is, Anangu engaged with settler economies in a way that provided access to commodities or cash but also allowed them to continue moving across ancestral country, visiting sites and spending time with kin.[48] Across Australia, missions were important sites for emphasising and instilling capitalist work ethic, 'labour as a calling', and often made rations conditional on labour, as part of the process of socialising people into waged work.[49] Anthropologist Diana Young concludes, '[B]etween the 1940s and the 1960s, [dingo] pupping was a perfect occupation for Anangu. There was no "boss" as there was in pastoral and mission work.'[50]

Pitjantjatjara woman Elsie, whose life story I recorded, holds memories of her father moving between work on arid pastoral stations and ceremonial life throughout the same period. She remembers her mother cooking damper for shearers. 'She'd make a lot of damper for them in the camp oven, she'd make a stew and all.'[51]

In cities, too, Aboriginal people found opportunities for work. Heidi Norman vividly evokes Redfern and surrounds during and after World War II. This inner-city locale was 'abuzz with factories and the railway yards', and Koori men and women easily found employment in chocolate factories, for Smith's Chips and in the railway yards, among other places.[52]

Finally, near Ceduna, Aboriginal men moved on and off the Koonibba mission, undertaking itinerant work around the district, as Bert, Vera,

Robby and others of their generation described to me. Aboriginal men across South Australia were 'forever on the move in search of work' and in the Ceduna region were railway workers, shearers, rouseabouts and fencers, as well as working on the wharves of the Ceduna–Thevenard deep-sea port, loading wheat and wool among other things.[53] Their families often lived in rudimentary reserves—the Ceduna reserve had no water—on the outskirts of relatively segregated rural towns and faced harassment from non-Aboriginal locals and authorities. In these harsh conditions, Bert's mum and others raised their children and maintained their pieced-together homes.

∴

I've braided together here stories usually told separately. First, there's the history of how those who either could not find, or could not do, waged work have been provided for over time. Not everyone was provided for as the Australian welfare state took shape during the twentieth century: Aboriginal people and other racialised groups were systematically excluded from access to some forms of social security, and their access to other forms was conditional.

This story is entangled with the history of an exploited and precarious Aboriginal labour force. Bark stripping; bean- and pea-picking; dogging; shearing: all point to a world of seasonal, mobile rural work. In the present, there is much discussion of the breakdown in stable working arrangements and the rise of casual and piecemeal work in Australia, some of it in dangerous gig economy occupations such as Uber delivery by bike. These Indigenous histories of precarious, unpredictable labour are an important reminder of the working conditions belonging especially to the post-war period and the welfare state's golden age. Secure work, the family wage derived from the Harvester judgment and designated leisure time were an aberration. This stable scenario was aberrant both in terms of human history and in terms of the small group of people around the world who reaped its benefits.

Importantly, the precarious patterns of work described above precluded the opportunity to amass, pass on and inherit wealth and have contributed to the poverty experienced by many First Nations people today. It was also working lives of this kind that were especially affected as the late twentieth century saw working conditions transformed across the Global North. I am referring not just to the process of deindustrialisation and the rise of a feminised service economy but also to the loss of jobs in rural areas as mechanised agribusiness usurped earlier forms of land use. Anthropologist Barry Morris describes a shift from Aboriginal 'underemployment to unemployment' on the New South Wales north coast, a process repeated in other similar regions.[54] This momentous period—beginning in the 1970s—is where I begin chapter 3.

Before the historical story continues, however, it is worth pausing to consider the implications of these historical stories. It might be tempting to seek to resuscitate earlier iterations of the Australian welfare state, in the wake of the series of punitive reforms that ensued from the 1990s onwards and which are detailed in this book. However, the history described here makes clear that this would entail longing for something that had racial exclusion and a patriarchal, heterosexual norm hard-baked into its design. The welfare state's past is not presented here as a template or object of nostalgia. Rather, a historically informed grasp of the present is necessary to envisage a new future and to find a better way to care for others.

3

Surveillance

The 1970s were famously transformative. By then, Aboriginal people were formally eligible to receive social security payments on the same basis as other Australians. Equal wages were also in effect. In 1975, the Whitlam government passed the *Racial Discrimination Act*. After its passage it became more difficult for state authorities to intervene, explicitly, in someone's intimate life on the basis of their Aboriginality. As well as raising social security rates for all beneficiaries and introducing no-fault divorce laws, the Whitlam government established the Supporting Mothers' Benefit for single mums, which is the predecessor of today's Parenting Payment (Single).[1]

The 1970s also saw global capitalism in the grip of a much-storied crisis. 'The global economic situation was characterised by the intractability of inflation and rising unemployment,' explains Elizabeth Humphrys.[2] Philip Mendes sheds light on the extent of the challenge in Australia. In 1971, annual welfare spending comprised 17.7 per cent of the budget. By 1981, it comprised 27.3 per cent; the 'major growth was in unemployment and sickness benefits'.[3]

The causes of this situation are complex. What's important for this story is the political response, which was naturalised and gained ascendency across Global North societies in the throes of deindustrialisation and with rising numbers of unemployed persons to support. This response is generally glossed as 'neoliberalism' and entailed 'deregulation, privatisation and withdrawal of the state from many areas of social provision'.[4] Labour movements were also defeated and their demands curtailed. Wage growth was effectively supressed and remains so.

These developments coincided with second-wave feminism's push for women's access to education and jobs outside the home. When I interviewed Ayesha about her experience of ParentsNext, she eloquently captured the extent of this transformation. Motherhood, she assured me, was 'a very fulfilling role'. She continued: 'But I'll be very honest, and I think I've admitted this to myself, as much as I love being a mum—and I love it more than anything—I need to be an active person, have the career as well.' The end of a public service contract coincided with the birth of Ayesha's daughter, and her relationship had since broken down. She reflected, 'I live and breathe for her, but I still need more.'[5]

Needing more than motherhood, in the form of paid work, evolved into a financial need, not just an existential one. Two incomes are critical to sustain life comfortably in a contemporary economy geared around dual-income households, especially amid wage stagnation and rocketing housing costs.

As unemployment rose in the 1970s, a new pejorative colloquialism emerged in Australia: 'dole bludger'. 'Bludger' was originally a nineteenth-century word for a sex worker's pimp, who carried a bludgeon. The pimp or bludger lived comfortably off the sex worker's labour. In the 1970s, 'dole bludgers' were increasingly cast as living off the hard work of the taxpayer, even compelling the taxpayer to keep working to keep society going and provide for the indolent poor. For historian Verity Archer, who traces this genealogy, the salient cultural distinction in Australia within debates about welfare since this time is not so much between the categories of deserving and undeserving poor as between welfare recipient and taxpayer.[6] The slur of 'bludger' remains in use today.

American political scientist Lawrence Mead's thinking on dependency was highly influential in Australian policy circles from the mid-1990s onwards.[7] Mead argues that individual welfare recipients are to blame for their own circumstances—not so much that it is their fault but that they are deficient as individuals, lacking 'mastery' over their own lives.[8] Mead advocated for what he called 'new paternalism': more supervisory and directive ways of governing the lives of the poor.[9]

In his own explanation of new paternalism, Mead describes the state acting as parent, envisaging a more authoritative government, which closely supervises its dependants. Misbehaviour is not just punished; it is pre-empted by the oversight of authority figures. Note the gendered metaphor here: this version of the welfare state should act as a kind of dominating father figure whose main task is to discipline. In fact, Mead makes clear that the new paternalism is a response to 1960s permissiveness, the dissolution of the nuclear family and the rise of single mother-headed households in the United States. Reinstalling patriarchal authority can therefore be understood as a key objective of the new paternalism.[10]

What ParentsNext crystallises, however, is that contemporary welfare policy does not envisage restoration of the idealised nuclear family belonging to the period before second-wave feminism. As explained in chapter 2, Australia's twentieth-century wage arbitration and welfare system were designed around a white male worker who provides for his dependants. Today, the Australian welfare state positions working women as ideal mothers. ParentsNext is underpinned by the assumption that impoverished women who stay home to raise their children need close monitoring lest they expect the state to support them for too long. I will return to this theme in chapter 5.

By the 1990s, across numerous countries in the Global North, welfare was loudly condemned as promoting 'parasitic' ways of life. Welfare receipt was seen to inhibit the 'development of the capacities requisite to proper personhood and citizenship, namely, independence, autonomy and self-sufficiency'. Dependency, as per Mead, was evoked as a deeply demeaning condition. Apparently beleaguered welfare states, it followed, were in urgent need of 'reform', which entailed 'liberation from welfare'.[11] Rapid restructuring of the architecture of the welfare state proceeded.

∴

Australia embarked on the privatisation of social security delivery earlier and more systematically than comparative polities. In the mid-1990s '[s]everal hundred for-profit and non-profit agencies were licensed to deliver case management services to the long-term unemployed'.[12] These agencies operated alongside the Commonwealth Employment Service (CES), which was a public labour exchange service established in the post-war period.[13] This essentially signalled the creation of a market, which has had several iterations since. The CES was dissolved completely in 2003.

The election of John Howard's coalition government in 1996 heralded further reform of the welfare system. The 'Coalition seemed to assume that many income security recipients were guilty of major character flaws unless proven innocent'.[14] Hostile talk led to concrete initiatives. Work for the Dole was introduced in 1997 and initially applied only to young unemployed people. Its application progressively expanded. In international parlance, Work for the Dole is 'workfare'. Importantly, those undertaking mandated activities such as Work for the Dole are legally defined as non-workers. This is 'despite the fact they may be labouring alongside "real workers" and perform the same and/or similar activities as those who receive a wage'. Where 'real workers' have legislative protections surrounding their health, safety, compensation and superannuation, non-workers remain outside these protections.[15]

The controversial Community Development Program (CDP) is a remote and more stringent Work for the Dole program. I spoke to numerous people in Ceduna who were subject to CDP as well as being on the card: they were eager to voice their contempt of this program, which is in the process of being rescinded and will be wound up in 2023. Like ParentsNext, the CDP has involved extremely high rates of social security payment suspension. Further, in the case of CDP and in contrast to ParentsNext, the accrual of suspensions has led to 'disengagement' from the welfare system.[16] That is, people end up in a situation where they might well have no independent source of income and whose basic needs for care, shelter and food are met by those around them.

To be clear, specific programs such as ParentsNext, Work for the Dole and CDP all fall under the banner of a more general bipartisan policy: 'mutual obligation'. At first glance, mutual obligation enshrines a commonly held conception of reciprocity: 'individuals should make a contribution to society in exchange for the support society gives them'.[17] Anthropologists have long been interested in practices of exchange, detailing the way gift-giving knits people together, reproducing open-ended relations of respect where the debt is never resolved.[18] Policy rhetoric, however, should not be confused with reality.

The 'support' Australian society grants an individual under the banner of mutual obligation comprises an inadequate income and the allocation of a frontline case manager at an employment services agency. Vital to grasp is the fact that these case managers have a 'dual role to play'.[19] Case managers must simultaneously seek to 'develop trusting, supportive relationships with vulnerable people' and to police 'them with potentially serious consequences, including loss of benefits payments for up to eight weeks'.[20] More simply put, case managers are charged with both helping and hassling their clients. Further, a payment-by-outcome marketised system means that people who require more intensive support and are less likely to attract a bonus for moving back into work, become unattractive clients, as these agencies seek ultimately to maximise profits.[21] Unemployed persons' activities have become an 'object of calculation and measure' like any other commodity.[22] The welfare state's gift of support, then, can be given in different ways. This is what sociologist Emma Mitchell refers to as the 'spirit' of 'mean welfare'.[23] 'Mutual obligation' does not enshrine honourable exchange.

••

So where does this leave the welfare state today? Much has been written about Clinton's 1996 welfare reforms, which thoroughly dismantled the cash support available to impoverished single mothers and their children in the United States.[24] Indeed, writing about the United States, sociologist Loïc Wacquant objects to the idea of welfare 'reform'. For Wacquant, rather than reforms, Clinton's initiative was part of a 'counter-revolution'—an explicit attack on the gains of the civil rights decades through welfare state restructuring, which has condemned poor Black women to low-wage, insecure work on the one hand and poor Black men to intensive policing and incarceration, on the other.[25] Regarding the United Kingdom, too, scholars write of welfare state retrenchment. Decades in the making, this process has intensified amidst austerity reforms.[26]

Examples abound that support the image of a meaner, leaner Australian welfare state. A vicious attack on welfare spending was a centrepiece of the Coalition's 2014 budget, for example. A headline-grabbing proposal first mooted in 2017—the widespread drug-testing of welfare recipients—enjoyed a long life as a policy prospect even if it was never introduced.[27] And there's the infamous automated debt recovery program, Robodebt, which targeted 'welfare fraud' to retrospectively recoup state spending that was allegedly illegitimate.

Journalist Martin McKenzie-Murray provides a heart-wrenching account of one of Robodebt's targets, detailing the circumstances surrounding Rhys Cauzzo's suicide. Cauzzo was a florist and musician. He also suffered from depression. McKenzie-Murray describes 'aggressive letters' sent to him by a debt collection agency engaged by the federal government to pursue an alleged Centrelink debt. The original debt was almost $18 000, which was quickly revised to around $10 000 without explanation. Both Cauzzo's mother and girlfriend believe the debt was a 'contributing factor' to his suicide a few weeks after the debt agency left a calling card for him at home.

Ultimately, however, Robodebt represented a failed attack on welfare recipients, although its damage to people's lives was far-reaching. Robodebt's broad target and crude method—averaging inconstant sources of income across a whole year—resulted in negative publicity surrounding the scheme's overreach. And, as it turned out, its illegality.[28] Those targeted by Robodebt, as well as families of victims, worked tirelessly both to contest debts and to generate public unease about the federal government's pursuit of these moneys.[29] Robodebt's victims were humanised in a range of media stories, although this might well be because many of them were no longer welfare recipients and some incurred their alleged debts as students receiving means-tested income support. Rather than recouping costs, the Morrison government ended up settling a class action for around $1.8 billion.[30]

Further, rather than a 'post-welfare' state, sociologist Ben Spies-Butcher convincingly terms this a 'dual welfare state', showing that many

Australians benefit through tax concessions that are not visible within public discourse as 'welfare'. Other more broadly targeted forms of welfare comprise subsidised childcare and the Family Tax Benefit. Both were critical to my survival when I studied for my PhD with two small children, living in an inner-city share house with my partner and friends. Yet I never imagined myself as 'welfare dependent' in this period. There are political consequences arising from this insulation of higher-income beneficiaries from the label of 'welfare': the middle class 'become fierce defenders' of the various forms of social spending they benefit from, allowing the spending on marginalised groups to further deteriorate.[31] Two categories of citizen, with vastly different political resources, are being effectively pitted against each other.

••

Journalist Nicolas Rothwell describes his encounter with a 'dog-eared document', eighty pages long, densely argued and faintly photocopied. It was an early version of Noel Pearson's *Our Right to Take Responsibility*, self-published in 2000 and republished in a 2009 collection of his writings. For Rothwell, this was a work of subtlety and originality, flecked with 'genius'.[32] Pearson's argument is essentially that welfare moneys and drinking have steadily eroded the quality of daily life in remote Aboriginal Australia since the advent of equal rights—both to the provisions of the welfare state and to legally consume alcohol. He describes Aboriginal society on Cape York as 'dysfunctional'.[33]

Pearson argues that in the pre-colonial period Aboriginal people partook of a 'real economy', in which the labour involved in food procurement was crucial to the reproduction of Indigenous society. 'You don't work, you starve,' Pearson states. Post-invasion (my term, not his), Aboriginal people also engaged in waged labour, as described in chapter 2, or work was demanded from them on missions, in exchange for rations. In the 'whitefella market economy', the reality is equally stark: 'You don't work, you don't get paid.'[34] However, since the 1970s welfare payments have come to replace both waged work and the pre-colonial work essential to subsistence, observes Pearson. Pearson describes this as 'passive welfare' and argues that the flow of these moneys into Cape York communities has corrupted the cultural obligation to share, so that resources are collectivised and then drained by problem drinkers.

For Pearson, 'passive welfare' erodes responsibility and reciprocity: payments are made absent any transaction. The recipient is not 'required to work or to provide anything in return'.[35] Note here the resonances with the concept of 'mutual obligation': historian Tim Rowse argues that both the mainstream government policy of 'mutual obligation' and Pearson's diagnosis of the problems with 'passive welfare' have in common the assumption that social security recipients are at risk of entrenched social exclusion and posit increased expectations of 'participation' as a remedy. There are also important divergences, especially in the institutional arrangements proposed to facilitate increased participation.[36] Pearson understands the era of universal access to social security to have installed a new relationship between a local Cape York welfare recipient and a distant source of resources: the Commonwealth Government. The government, however, has no moral authority, unlike senior community figures. Thus, cultural structures are undermined, inhibiting possibilities for self-determined futures. Pearson envisages restoration of intra-community moral relations.

Other close observers of Cape York life have questioned Pearson's 'mono-causal' account of the troubling conditions in Cape York communities, whereby the introduction of the welfare-based cash economy alone precipitated the emergence of today's problems.[37] As well as pointing to a conjunction of historical and economic factors, others have complicated Pearson's portrait of pre-1970s community life there. Pearson's vision of an abstemious, industrious and domesticated people risks extrapolating from the experience of authoritarian supervision on the Lutheran mission of Hope Vale to all mission and pastoral communities in Cape York, 'to provide an all-encompassing theory of social change since the 1970s'.[38]

While Lawrence Mead's thinking certainly influenced Pearson, some historians posit that Pearson advanced a more nuanced and Indigenous-specific conception of paternalism. Ben Silverstein and Claire McLisky carefully argue that Pearson's writings calling for the restitution of 'paternalist structures' have been misunderstood as a call for a return to white authority. Rather than assuming that paternalism is synonymous with a 'blunt exercise of power', these historians perceive that Pearson was seeking to reinstate a particular experience of paternalism as a system of reciprocity and relationality, in which a more powerful 'patron' offers mentoring and guidance. While undeniably 'asymmetrical', this model of paternalism demands mutual transformation rather than elimination.[39]

Another feature of Pearson's argument is worth dwelling on. When he writes of the 'real labour' belonging to pre-contact times, he counters those 'lies' so injurious to Robby in the opening of chapter 2. There was activity here, says Pearson. People worked. Through Bruce Pascoe's *Dark Emu*, a broad public audience has learned more about manifold forms of pre-contact labour, which included hunting, food collecting, eel- and fish-trapping and working with fire to shape landscapes.[40]

In the Australian settler colonies, 'work' became something narrowly and less relationally defined to refer primarily to male waged work, devaluing caring and domestic activities in the process and erasing First Nations labour. Thinking of and acknowledging work in these narrow terms remains a striking feature of our society, even if it is now not just men who are expected to undertake this kind of valorised work. However, perhaps something is lost also if in recognising these skilled Indigenous undertakings that were previously invisible to outsiders, these actions are too quickly absorbed into the imposed category of work. Presence on country, sweating on country, ceremony on country: all these forms of attentiveness are just as necessary for keeping country 'sweet', happy and fecund as more practical and everyday efforts to sustain country and life.[41]

∴

In the dying days of John Howard's long period of political rule, a sweeping intervention was launched in the Northern Territory with the stated aim of 'normalising' Aboriginal community life there. It was as part of this suite of legislation that compulsory income management was introduced to the Territory in 2007 and then in designated Cape York communities in 2008.[42] The *Racial Discrimination Act 1975* was suspended in order to facilitate this, well, racially discriminatory policy.

Compulsory income management at this time generally involved 50 per cent of an affected social security recipient's income being quarantined on to a BasicsCard so that it could not be spent on alcohol, gambling, tobacco and pornography products. The lime-green BasicsCard was designed to be used at stores licensed to accept it.

Income management in Cape York was and remains different from income management in the Territory. In Cape York, a Family Responsibility Commission (FRC), comprising local senior figures and others, assumes a state-like role and becomes intimately involved in governing others' lives, as they make decisions about who is in need of a BasicsCard and what proportion of their social security payments should be quarantined. The Cape York Welfare Reform Trial explicitly targets specific behaviour, potentially quarantining the benefits of community members who are: the subject of a child safety concern; have not enrolled their child in school or failed to send them to school for three days without a reasonable excuse; have committed a petty crime; or have violated a public housing tenancy agreement.[43] Assessment of the effects of the Cape York initiatives have been mixed, but analysts note that the 'positive outcomes' attributed to it are 'linked to the specific model and not income management per se'.[44] It seems the guidance and mentorship that Silverstein and McLisky identify as a positive possibility of paternalism is a factor here. I am pointing out that this is a slightly different policy experiment, with slightly different ideas animating it.

By the end of 2007, Howard was out of office and the Labor government was anxious to reinstate the *Racial Discrimination Act*. Income management was first expanded beyond Indigenous communities within the Northern Territory to affect non-Indigenous Territorians. Then 2012 saw a further extension of the BasicsCard to a series of disadvantaged postcodes across Australia. In fact, it has proved infrequently issued outside the Territory: as of June 2022, there were almost 23 000 people with a BasicsCard in the Territory and around 1600 people with a BasicsCard living across the rest of Australia.⁴⁵ In sum, the BasicsCard presages the cashless debit card, introduced around a decade later. How did this even more contentious card come about? The short answer is this: Andrew Forrest dreamed it up. A longer, more circuitous explanation follows.

••

If the American south-western cities of Salt Lake City, Albuquerque, Phoenix and Los Angeles were to occupy the cardinal points on a map, in between them lies resource-rich Navajo land. Yet Navajo people find themselves in a state of destitution. Why? This story is a familiar one. Navajo herds were destroyed through a contest over water sources in which ranchers usurped their resources. Later, coal-mining began, which promised independence but in fact created little in the way of economic opportunity for Navajo and saw them saddled with the residue of nitrous oxide, fly ash and mercury emissions.⁴⁶

It's not just the loss of resources and overblown promises of the benefits associated with involvement in mining that strike me as familiar. High-voltage transmission power lines now connect Navajo lands to south-western cities located in deserts made more habitable because of the advent of air-conditioning. Historian Andrew Needham directs his readers to see a relationship we are not used to seeing, to train our eye on those power lines strung across the landscape.

In Australia, there is nothing so material that we can apprehend in order to grasp that those of us who lead comfortable lives are connected to—indeed are in some sense dependent upon—resources rightfully owned by Indigenous people. Put more explicitly, the unevenly shared wealth of this nation state is substantially generated from the extraction of resources from lands subject to Indigenous interests. At the height of the last mining boom, a surge so strong it insulated Australia from the worst effects of the 2008–09 global financial crisis, 'up to 60 per cent of the country's export income … came from mining'.⁴⁷ To focus on the problem that welfare beneficiaries are so readily accepted to represent provides a massive distraction from other kinds of problematic dependencies that cushion the lives of many Australians.

Much of this wealth has been generated in the iron ore-rich Pilbara, which is exported to China. And it is in the Pilbara that Andrew 'Twiggy' Forrest began to acquire vast mining tenements in the 2000s. Forrest's Fortescue Metals Group (FMG) is now among the most profitable mining companies in Australia. As his fortunes grew, so did Forrest's public profile. In 2020, Forrest delivered the nationally broadcast Boyer Lecture calling for ethical entrepreneurship and green energy.

Less well known is the fact that from 2007 FMG was engaged in a protracted legal struggle with the Yindjibarndi Aboriginal Corporation (YAC) over the country affected by FMG's Solomon Mine. The Yindjibarndi pursued here a form of native title called 'exclusive possession'—this would not have affected the mine but entitled compensation to be paid into a community benefit fund. FMG 'poured scorn on the need to pay compensation', which they consistently referred to as 'mining welfare'.[48] Yindjibarndi people ultimately prevailed, an extraordinary feat given FMG's 'extreme and aggressive' conduct throughout.[49] More specifically, FMG resourced a rival Yindjibarndi group, staging sham meetings as part of its efforts to undermine the YAC's position.[50]

Just the kind of guy, then, that Tony Abbott's federal government should select to advise them on Aboriginal employment policy. Yes, FMG claims it has consistently maintained high levels of Aboriginal employment at its mines, which is a complicated matter; Indigenous employment targets often fall short at other mines.[51] Yet this fact alone hardly qualifies and equips Forrest to design large-scale social policy.

In 2014, *The Forrest Review: Creating Parity* was released. Parity in employment outcomes was the stated objective. However, outside the remit of this review, Forrest also argued for the implementation of a drastic welfare measure. Forrest urged the immediate implementation of a scheme whereby 'an individual's welfare payments … would be paid into a savings account drawn on with a Healthy Welfare Card'.[52] This card would be blocked from the purchase of designated substances at the point of sale, through the Electronic Financial Transfer at Point of Sale (EFTPOS) system. The 'Healthy Welfare Card' idea morphed into the reality of the cashless debit card.

The cashless debit card and the BasicsCard are often confused in public debates about income management. Both are examples of income management. The differences are these: the cashless debit card was more stringent than the BasicsCard, in terms of the greater percentage of payments quarantined as a default—80 per cent rather than 50 per cent. Funds quarantined on to the cashless debit card could not be spent on alcohol and gambling products; funds quarantined on to the BasicsCard cannot be spent on alcohol, gambling products, cigarettes or pornography.

The cashless debit card also relied on different technology. The cashless debit card blocked merchant codes at the point of sale; wherever an EFTPOS terminal was installed, the card should, in theory, have functioned. Whereas EFTPOS terminals are ubiquitous across Australia, the BasicsCard works only at stores approved for its use.

The process leading up to the cashless debit card's introduction in Ceduna in March 2016 is described in more detail in chapter 4. I hand over to my interviewees to tell this story from their perspective. In April 2016, it was introduced in the East Kimberley. The card's introduction to community life in the East Kimberley seems to have been especially 'chaotic'.[53]

A third trial of the card commenced in the Goldfields region of Western Australia in March 2018. While the vast majority of cardholders in Ceduna and the East Kimberley were Indigenous, as of mid-2022, 49 per cent of the participants in the Goldfields trial were Indigenous.[54] A fourth trial was rolled out in Hervey Bay and Bundaberg, Queensland, from January 2019. In this predominantly non-Indigenous trial site, the card was compulsorily issued to a more specific subset of social security recipients: those aged 35 and under on specific income support payments. The political discourse about the card here shifted to an emphasis on youth unemployment and intergenerational welfare as well as social harm.[55]

In late 2020, the Morrison government moved to make all four 'trials' permanent—two of these trials had by then been going for close to five years. There was also a plan to transition all BasicsCard users to the cashless debit card. Debate of this bill was heated. 'Try living the life of a person on this card,' Yawuru Labor Senator Patrick Dodson challenged the chamber.[56] Ultimately, independent Senator Rex Patrick decided to vote with Labor against the plan, citing concerns that 'the data is not there that supports that … the card achieves what it is intended to achieve'.[57]

All four of the extant cashless debit card trials were instead legislated to conclude at the end of 2022. In addition, BasicsCard users in the Northern Territory and Cape York were given the option to switch to a cashless debit card. This is where the situation stood before the 2022 federal election.

∴

So far, I have characterised both ParentsNext and the card as examples of 'punitive' and ever more 'conditional' welfare. In closing this chapter, I want to be more precise about the nature of these two examples of conditional welfare.

There is a key difference between the individual's responsibility to adhere to conditions under ParentsNext on the one hand and the way conditions are pre-emptively enforced via income management on the other. In the main, conditional welfare initiatives organised under the general banner of mutual obligation, such as ParentsNext or Work for the Dole, rest on a system of individual compliance. The recipient's adherence to a set of often tailored conditions is digitally monitored. Breaches or alleged breaches of conditions result in the application of individual sanctions. All this is to instil a sense of personal responsibility and discipline believed to be lacking. The anxiety and atmosphere of threat instilled by this enforcement system is described by my interviewees in the chapters to come.

Income management, however, organises the conditions attached to the receipt of social security payments pre-emptively. In keeping with Mead's theory of new paternalism, the cashless debit card was designed to predict and prevent 'bad behaviour' on the part of the cardholder, rather than incentivise 'responsible behaviour' as mandated participation in ParentsNext activities putatively does. Blanket conditions were applied to broad categories of income support payment recipients. As one person subject to the card correctly perceived, 'It's as if we are [all] being punished for somebody else's bad behaviour.'

Adherence to income management conditions is designed to be automatically facilitated by technological instruments. Cashless debit cardholders were therefore prevented from spending a designated proportion of their quarantined social security moneys on prohibited items. Breaching these conditions involved engaging in collective or individual workarounds entirely outside and beyond any monitoring regime. In chapter 4 I explore various ways locals devised to get around the card's conditions in Ceduna. Because these everyday strategies to work around the card occurred outside the administration of social security, there was no sanction regime in place.

∴

This abridged history of the Australian welfare state delivers the story up to mid-2022. The remainder of the book is devoted to delving into people's experience of life on welfare. Their voices carry the story forward.

PART 2
Life on welfare

4

'Stressed out to be on the card'

'When did you first hear about the cashless debit card?' I asked people in Ceduna. These are some of the responses I recorded: 'They were sending that piece of paper out in the mail.' And, 'I got it!' One person narrated, 'Came back from Queensland, wanted to work and had to go on Newstart.' Then, 'They said, "Oh, when you go on Newstart, you have to go on Indue Card."' This person's response? 'I said, "You're joking?" They said, "No." Fuck me dead! It's the truth!'

∴

Robby was posted his lead-pencil grey card. It resembled a Visa card but had the Indue logo also printed on it. When he received it, he couldn't bring himself to handle it. He said, 'Soon as I got it, I just didn't touch it for about—I don't know—about two payments.' He was receiving fortnightly unemployment payments at the time. For a month, he subsisted on the funds remaining in his bank account. Craig, a whitefella, also refused to use his card until he too started to run out of money.

The cashless debit card was an object: plastic, brittle, fairly nondescript but potent in its meanings. It was an 'artefact', as anthropologist Cameo Dalley identifies.[1] Robby avoided contact with a thing that gave material reality to a humiliating intervention in his circumstances, as he experienced it. Craig also told me about a friend of his who snipped theirs up.

In Ceduna, the card was known as the 'grey card', after its appearance; the 'Indue card', after the company that was contracted to issue and administer the card; and occasionally 'welfare card', which derives from Andrew Forrest's original proposal. In the East Kimberley, the card was referred to as the 'white card', as it was imposed by white people and reflected white designs. This moniker emerged within weeks of its introduction there.[2]

When I asked people in Ceduna when they first heard about the cashless debit card, they often talked of it arriving in the mail, as suggested above. However, some people first read about the card in the local paper before its introduction. This short news story set in train a series of events contesting the implementation of the first cashless debit card trial.

••

In August 2015, the *West Coast Sentinel* featured a series of colour images, spread across multiple pages. These showed the signing of a Memorandum of Understanding between the federal government, the Ceduna District Council and five Aboriginal organisations. The accompanying article stated, 'The introduction of a Cashless Debit Card Trial in Ceduna from February [2016] has received an optimistic response from community members with most agreeing it could be the solution to continuing alcohol and drug abuse issues.' The then Far West Community Heads Group spokesperson, the late Mick Haynes, was quoted at length: 'We want to build a future for our younger generation to aspire to and believe we cannot do this if our families are caught up in a destructive cycle of alcohol or drugs that destroys our culture, our lands and our communities.' He continued, 'As local leaders we want to champion the cause for the betterment of our people and believe this will benefit the region as a whole.'[3]

A week earlier, a short ABC news article had outlined the origins of the trial in the Forrest Report, emphasising that Ceduna had a problem with alcohol-related violence and illness. That article read, 'The Government said the card would not be aimed at the Indigenous community and would affect all welfare recipients in the areas that are subject to the trial.'[4]

The appearance of the *Sentinel* story stirred a handful of people into action, eager to dispute the depiction of exhaustive consultation and community involvement in decision-making. 'None of those government officials ever spoken to the community. It's like they was all cherrypicked,' it was said to me. 'The mayor, he picked the people that favoured the card, so the government officials spoke to the people that favoured the card.'

Another expressed it this way: 'They pulled the blanket over everyone and just secretly said that everyone is on the card, without informing the community about it.' And again: 'No one was told about it. It was all very underhanded and sneaky.' One Aboriginal person questioned whether 'hand-picked' leaders were really 'mingling' with the community, another expressed cynicism about the mantle of 'community leader', and one voiced frustration about those who would 'sit in offices' making decisions, suggesting they do so at some remove from the exigencies and struggles of community life.

These stories deserve capture and are important to reckon with. 'They are not talking to the little people,' came one person's evocative summing up. Beyond disempowerment, this genre of comments also points to a less obvious theme: the exalted status of 'consultation' in political life, which has consequences for the kinds of political demands articulated.

∴

Since the Intervention launched by the Howard government in 2007, Indigenous policy has been characterised by an increasingly coercive and carceral approach.[5] Consultation and the more sophisticated process of policy 'co-design' came to seem like watchwords of a past, more liberal era, which purported to honour Aboriginal community aspirations and foster involvement. However, the neat image of policy eras obscures a messier and less coherent reality.[6] The past is not clearly broken with: consultation, and dedicated participation in the rituals that are supposed to evidence it, was clearly considered imperative in order to legitimise the introduction of the card—itself a coercive, illiberal measure. Rote consultation processes with predetermined outcomes are a hallmark of the contemporary university, and I am depressingly familiar with them. One effect of their constancy is that demands for 'more consultation' and 'real consultation' are asserted in response: a narrow political vision assumes prominence.

So, to be clear: Forrest generated the idea, which drew on a broader global policy logic and language of dependency, discipline, behaviour change and the need to reform welfare. In an interview, I asked one of the card's most prominent and powerful proponents about the origins of the card. My interviewee immediately nominated the moment he read an opinion piece by Forrest in the *Australian* around the time of the Forrest Report's release. 'Canberra' then pursued the possibility of putting this idea into practice. What happened next?

I interviewed Pam, who was intimately involved in the local processes that took place in the year between the release of the Forrest Report in August 2014 and the August 2015 announcement of the cashless debit card trial in Ceduna. 'I'm very proud of the work we did. I don't think people understood the amount of consultation we did,' she told me. In that year, she drove between the region's localities 'constantly'. Pam reminisced, 'Backwards and forwards, backwards and forwards. I would attend every community meeting, every board meeting. Any kind of meeting … I'd be in there.' She put up with a lot of 'shit': anger borne of confusion, as she understood it. 'And I kept coming back and I kept coming back.'

What I see unfolding is this: Pam is describing having worked hard at her job and a process she believed in. She also hoped, more 'personally', in the card's potential to arrest the wreckage alcohol and drug addiction leave in its wake. Importantly, however, Pam is essentially describing the dogged persistence with which a pre-existing concept—the card—was set before those community members who were in a position to attend community and board meetings. While Pam stressed to me that the policy was 'co-designed', this in fact seems to refer only to a slight but significant tweaking of what Forrest originally proposed. An entirely cashless system, as the Healthy Welfare Card envisaged, was deemed unworkable. The split of restricting 80 per cent of an affected payment onto a card and 20 per cent remaining unrestricted and being paid into an ordinary bank account was arrived at. The term 'co-design' should rightfully refer to a 'bottom-up process whereby policy-makers partner as equals with excluded groups'. Co-design as Pam uses the term is a misnomer here. Like the BasicsCard before it, analysts conclude, the card was fundamentally 'top-down'.[7]

••

In response to the August 2015 *Sentinel* article, a small group of locals arranged for a public meeting to take place in a function room at the Foreshore Hotel in the month following the agreement's signing. About thirty people, Aboriginal and non-Aboriginal, old and young, went along— 'the biggest variety of people'. 'We tried to get the mayor to come,' I was told. 'We give them all invitations to come. "This is your community people here: we want answers. We want a consultation, that we were never given." But no, we were on our own.' Another relayed, 'Basically the feeling was: how could this go on without us … knowing? Without talking to people about it?' Two more meetings organised by concerned locals followed.

The journalist George Megalogenis describes those Australian regional and rural areas that have largely been bypassed by two decades of skilled migration, especially from China and South Asia, as being 'older and whiter than the nation at large', warning that Australia risks a split 'between those who are globally connected and those who are yelling stop'.[8] Megalogenis has in mind the populist movements that fuelled Trump's election, the advent of Brexit and Pauline Hanson's political resurrection. I certainly encountered traces of those currents in Ceduna, in terms of distrust of public institutions and the professional classes: journalists, politicians and academics. But other grassroots political possibilities are evident in this town among disenfranchised people: here a tenuous alliance of affected citizens against the card seeded new friendships. 'It did bring the Aborigines and the whites closer because we were working together with a single aim,' said one opponent of the card.

On 15 October 2015 federal legislation implementing the card passed the Senate. It was only after the card had been legislated that a widely publicised public meeting was held at a local football club. This one was attended by the federal Human Services Minister at the time, Alan Tudge.

Not everyone knew about this meeting either. They were perhaps in the situation that a profoundly isolated middle-aged white man described to me: 'I was that out of touch, honestly. I have no communications. Apparently there was marches, there was rallies, there was everything, I didn't go to one of them ... That's what happens with poor people and I guarantee there's probably a thousand more that were like me.' Nonetheless, a large and animated gathering ensued down at the footy club.

The perceived contempt shown to a senior Aboriginal figure at that meeting made a deep impression on a number of my interviewees: 'Mr Tudge was so rude. He was so rude to that lady and she's an Aboriginal elder, she's really high up in their hierarchy. I had never seen anybody ... He just totally ignored her. It was just awful.' Sure, meeting attendees rambled, were nervous or furious, says another. But they were there to express themselves, it is remembered. A number of interviewees recall that government visitors, some of them advisers in their twenties, stood at the back of the venue with their arms crossed, 'snickering' at the contributions of local attendees.

Two weeks later came a protest organised by card opponents. 'We marched on the main street!' I was told proudly. Banners at this protest stated, 'We need rehab here' and 'Human rights, lost cause'.[9]

The card was rolled out in March 2016. Tudge and the then Prime Minister Malcolm Turnbull visited Ceduna in October 2016, six months after the trial commenced. The pair were greeted by more hand-painted banners: 'Black and White Together' and 'I'm not a Drunk'.[10] Turnbull 'turned his back' on them, it was remembered to me bitterly. I interviewed an assured and charismatic Aboriginal man, who spent time with Turnbull on that whirlwind visit. His summing up was this: '[I]t was like all this energy and effort being pushed into making something sound like it's working, when it's not.'

The initial trial of the card in Ceduna and the East Kimberley ran for around twelve months. In April 2017, these two trials were extended; at this stage, a government-commissioned evaluation report was pending. In February 2018, fierce parliamentary and public debate surrounded the first two trials, as the government sought both another extension and an expansion into a third locality. I was in Ceduna that searing hot summer and talked with June about the process. June, an Aboriginal grandmother and foster carer, who hated being on the card, perceived, 'Ah, they're sitting on it and then they'll say, "I've made up my mind, it's going through."' June was right: the two trials were extended again until June 2019. Further, a third trial in Western Australia's goldfields was added and commenced in March 2018.

The following year, the fourth and largest trial commenced in Queensland. So, by late 2020, when the government unsuccessfully proposed making all four trials permanent, Ceduna had been a cashless debit card 'trial site' for almost five years. In addition to the extension of the card's operation in the four sites until the end of 2022, another change was passed. The word 'trial' was replaced with 'program'.[11]

∴

'I had alcohol problems in the past,' began Dustin. Around two decades ago, Dustin's dad was killed in an accident. 'That really took a big effect,' he described—on himself, his siblings and on his mum. 'Alcohol was a depressant; I can't even remember six years of my life. I basically drank my life away.'

Then, 'As I got older I thought, "Nah, it's time to change and come to reality and deal with the emotional traumas." Because I've never seek no counselling for my father's death. My mum was always my counsellor.'

Dustin's dad had worked for a government department. And, 'On the weekends he loved his beers.' His sudden death, 'that really messed us up'. Dustin continued, 'My father, he was a hard-working man.'

At 15, Dustin announced, 'Dad, I'm dropping out of school.' And, 'he basically let me. But he made us get into work.' At this stage, the Community Development Employment Projects scheme (CDEP), which ran from 1977 to 2015, provided for community-directed employment projects. After a construction course, Dustin joined a building team. 'All the drop-outs back in that time, we all had opportunities to go to work.' Another Aboriginal man I talked with mused that he used to 'aspire' to be a part of CDEP; their work was respected when it resulted in housing and the upkeep of valued local facilities. Positive memories of the CDEP era, which effectively devolved power to local bodies, persist throughout remote Aboriginal Australia.[12]

Dustin often talked to me of his childhood. Out bush, he scrambled up trees to find the nests of waltja (wedge-tailed eagles) and in order to gaze down from above. He had a fascination with reptiles. Still does.

Again and again, Dustin returned to the moment that ruptured his life story: '… right up until when my father got killed … [T]hat really messed my life up a bit.' He remembered, 'All us kids, we just sort of wasn't on track. Sort of wasn't coping … I was always depressed and crying and my brother was just angry all the time.'

These days, Dustin told me, 'I can deal with my past problems, I can deal with just about every problem I ever went through.' Then again, 'When the card popped up here, that was sort of a problem, too. It sort of did bring on mental stressing and stress people out. A lot of people are stressed out to be on the card.'

∴

In Ceduna, hot northerly winds blow gritty sand off the desert. Topsoil is lifted off wheat paddocks and swirls thickly. On other days, I gulp air smelling of seaweed and brine: freezing southern seas stretch away. Why was the card first trialled here, at the continent's edge? This seems a place of extremes: marginal, harsh environs and confronting social circumstances. Recall Haynes's comments about the devastation wreaked by alcohol, which are borne out by statistics, experience and recent history.[13] 'Funeral after funeral,' muttered an old friend, whom I bumped into outside the Lutheran church one morning. 'I'm over it.'

When I say this is not a story about a particular place, I risk under-emphasising the geographical distribution of contemporary inequalities. Place-based realities matter. In Australia, transformations to rural and pastoral economies, which coincided with the introduction of equal wages, have seen many Aboriginal men especially lose their toehold in economic life. Aunty Vera and Uncle Bert's memories illustrate this.

Further, being in place involved being taught to see things with local eyes and to look more deeply into the suffering that shocking statistics seem to illustrate but do little to explain. Startling rates of admission to the sobering-up centre likely reflect a much smaller number of people's resourceful and habitual use of a facility with a warm bed and a washing machine, I was told. When I asked Rex if he agreed with the idea that since the introduction of the card things were 'quieter' (a euphemism deployed locally to refer to less public drinking), his response challenged the very terms of my question. Rex told me that 'a lot of our people are transient … or travellers. So, things might look quiet one minute and then they're full on the next, you know? And so, when we see things like that happening, that's what it is. It's not like, "Oh, it's working because it's quiet." We'd usually say, "It's quiet. Must be people gone somewhere, you know. Where've they all gone?" And then all of a sudden, they're all back.'

Beyond the particularity of places, in a settler colonial society, marginal and markedly Aboriginal locales serve as testing grounds for initiatives that are destined to operate more broadly. Achilles Mbembe sets this out: 'In fact, in most instances, the selection of races, the prohibition of mixed marriages, forced sterilization, even the extermination of vanquished peoples are to find their first testing ground in the colonial world.'[14] More specifically, IndigenousX founder Luke Pearson identified the cashless debit card as a welfare reform experiment that first affected mostly Aboriginal people before being generalised and coming to affect non-Aboriginal others, an insight that was especially true of the card's extension into Queensland. 'White Australia has long believed that the mistreatment of Indigenous Australians could never be perpetrated against them,' writes Pearson. He continues, '[B]ut we are already seeing this happen with cashless welfare cards being rolled out to non-Indigenous people … and other punitive measures that were first trialled on Indigenous people. The denial of rights that Indigenous people never even got the chance to enjoy is now plaguing the rest of the country as well.'[15]

∵

Helen welcomed me into her crafty, comfortable home. An ageing white woman on a Disability Support Pension, her complex physical problems derive from the many years she spent with an abusive husband, who is still alive and knows where she lives. She slid the bolt into the door behind me.

Helen commented that my visit was good timing: she was eager to tell me the following story. Just the day before, her card was rejected five times at the post office as she tried to pay her domiciliary care bill. At first, Helen thought the chip in her card might be damaged, but the post office worker assured her this just happens sometimes. She tried again without success.

Helen continued to the chemist but baulked at the idea of her card being rejected there; she used the cash component of her payment to buy her meds. Then she decided to delay her grocery shopping until another day and returned home. 'It's the trepidation,' Helen explained.

Helen was not the only person to talk to me about practical problems with the card. Uncle Clive travelled everywhere with 'two cards', he explained to me: his cashless debit card and his bank card. At a car mechanic's garage, his card was once declined, but he switched to his bank card. He has reserves. 'I've been in the workforce since I was 15; I don't need anyone telling me how to manage my money.' Carrying the card, Uncle Clive added, reminded him of accompanying his mother on the mission to collect their tea leaves and flour.

'My childcare fees: I can't pay them with a card,' Stacey explained to me. Stacey is a white woman, born and raised in Ceduna, who was working in aged care, studying and raising young children alone when I met up with her. She had 'income coming in', she assured me. As a single mother on a low wage, she was also entitled to additional state support. Every time she paid her childcare bill, 'I've got to ring up Indue.' She elaborated, 'You've got certain times to do it in. And at other times it don't work. If I can't get them in my lunch break, I've got to take time off work. I'm losing money just to make a phone call and try to get in contact with them.' She described the process, 'And then for me to get my bill paid, I've got to fax, send or email my bill to them for them to be able to access my funds to pay for it.'

'Before this card come into place,' Kelli-Anne complained, 'it was very easy for me to order my parts from eBay online. As soon as the card came in, I've tried to order parts, it doesn't work.' Because the purchase of alcohol is possible on eBay and its merchant code reflects this, the cashless debit card was blocked from working on eBay. The local repair places were busy when I talked to Kelli-Anne, a fiery and impressive Aboriginal woman: she preferred to source parts and fix vehicles herself.

I could keep listing the practical problems people shared with me and were determined, as Helen was, to have documented: the card not working—on occasion, at random—at the supermarket and at Port Augusta's bargain store, Cheap As Chips; the time the whole town was without power, the EFTPOS terminals were disabled and the supermarket would only accept cash. The $130 that remained on one man's cashless debit card at the time of the Oyster Festival. There was nothing in his account and his children couldn't go on the rides. They started crying. And there's one last story I feel both compelled to include and unsure about including: many people I spoke with insisted money was going missing from their accounts.

Tentatively, I floated the idea of looking into this further, which would need to begin with me browsing mysterious transactions to try to understand what was happening. People were understandably reluctant to embark upon this investigation. Card users' financial dealings were often not private from Indue, as Stacey's story reveals. At least they could decide to keep them private from a 'university lady'.

Some people were convinced that fellow cardholders had memorised others' details, which they gleaned from the frequent use of public computers in one another's presence. Perhaps they then logged on to accounts other than their own, in order to transfer money between cards? Many, however, were deeply suspicious of Indue: perhaps it was this company 'stealing' from accounts. I came to see that there was a deeper truth to this accusation, beyond the matter of whether the issue of 'missing' moneys was empirically true (and I certainly can't substantiate it). The accusation makes sense in two ways.

First, a corporation profited through its involvement in the finances of those reliant on welfare. It is worth hearing this as a nascent moral critique of the contemporary, marketised welfare system. Indue is a public, unlisted company, which specialises in financial products. In issuing and facilitating the workings of Indue cards in the cashless debit card sites, it made money from administering the finances of people living in extreme poverty. The cost associated with Indue's contract reportedly averaged out at $10 000 per participant in the first year of its operation. The cost dropped over time and in 2022 stood at $1100 per participant.[16] However, the $10 000 figure was widely report, circulated on social media and discussed.[17] Ten grand is insignificant to someone earning as much as, say, an Australian vice chancellor, but it is serious bunda (money) to the likes of Dustin, Kelli-Anne, Stacey, Uncle Clive and Helen.

Second and relatedly, this perception of missing moneys makes sense because the incomes of those living on welfare in Australia are insufficient and result in grinding poverty. Being compulsorily issued, the card did not reduce anyone's social security payments. But there are not enough funds in these bank accounts: they empty too quickly. It does not seem surprising or a misdiagnosis to point to 'missing' money.

∙∙

I chatted with Chazzy, an Aboriginal woman I had come to know quite well: we'd had numerous conversations about art, bush foods, raising kids and other topics. Chazzy told me casually she liked organising her finances online via her Indue account. The app was handy. I wanted to hear more, but that's all there was to it. Chazzy had a better idea. Rather than waste my time with her, she promised to introduce me to an uncle of hers who was 'very vocal' and locally well known for his opposition to the card. I could not convince her that her acceptance of the card was just as interesting to me as her uncle's problems with it.

When I talked to people about life on the cashless debit card, they were often careful to point out that they did not assume the right to speak for others. This was not just because it is culturally inappropriate to impinge on one's capacity to speak for oneself in this setting. Those on the card argued that they had been 'tarred with the same brush'. By contrast, they avoided generalising about their fellow community members—respecting the fact that everybody has the right to speak for themselves and tell their own story. 'Some like it,' I was frequently told. Like Chazzy, those who accepted the card often didn't have much to say about why, but I did collect some more detailed explanations.

Kieran's view on the card shifted from positive to ambivalent within our conversation. 'In all fairness, it probably has curbed my habits,' he stated. 'But then again,' he rushed on, 'maybe I was better off with cash because I used to go down the pub, knowing that I wasn't gonna get any more income, and I'd go and put a couple of bets on, on the horses. And I may just come out with a couple extra bucks, you know? I don't think that that's a bad thing, however, trying to do it with your last couple of dollars.'

Tynisha perceived that it was easier to save funds on the card: 'I can save up on that Indue card. Keep saving. Saving up.' Another told me: 'The Indue card is the greatest thing. I get paid Friday and I'm usually broke Saturday. At least with this thing, the money's still in the card.' Yet for others it interrupted established patterns of saving rather than creating new ones. 'Have a problem spending it quick. When I have cash, I normally save it. From my Indue, spend it real quick.' I asked why that was.

'Because it's different.'

When we first spoke at length, Gladys was unhappy about the card. I nattered with her again one day, sitting on her front steps, as I waited to take her nephew for a driving lesson. She told me it was getting 'used to it': 'That's all it was,' she surmised. A community worker expressed this in more political terms: Aboriginal people are 'used to being told what to do', she pointed out. 'It is no longer an issue,' she concluded. 'We get on with it.'

Normalisation or 'getting used to it' is not a straightforward process, it seems to me. Is it a matter of people becoming accustomed to something imposed and adjusting to the new reality of the card, or is it a matter of the card itself being creatively and effectively incorporated into community life, so that the card is itself absorbed into the pre-existing reality? The card imagined and treated welfare recipients as highly individuated persons with little understanding of the ways in which 'cash and resources move between Aboriginal people'.[18] Yet the card proved fungible. Cards were frequently shared. A grandmother and revered artist relayed an amusing story of going to pay her car registration and finding her card balance exactly one dollar short of the amount needed. She swapped cards with her daughter temporarily to pay the bill before they swapped back.

At first glance the mixed responses I documented echo the findings of the evaluation undertaken of the first year of the card's operation in Ceduna, which was released in August 2017. This evaluation was conducted by a private research company called ORIMA. Six months after the card was introduced into Ceduna, 49 per cent of the cardholders in Ceduna and the East Kimberley surveyed by ORIMA answered that the card had made their lives worse. Nine months later, this had dropped to 32 per cent. Across the two sites, the proportion reporting that the card had made their lives better remained consistent: 22 per cent at the six-month mark and 23 per cent at the 15-month mark. Further, 28 per cent of Ceduna participants reported a positive impact on their wellbeing, which was a far higher figure than the 18 per cent of participants in the East Kimberley.[19]

How then to account for these divergences? A common discursive strategy of card proponents was to argue that when those surveyed stated it had made their lives worse, this indicated that addicts' desires were being thwarted: the card was working.[20] Opposition to the card was also consistently besmirched. For example, in 2018, the federal member for Grey, Rowan Ramsey, told the House of Representatives that he remembered once speaking to Ceduna's mayor. He had noticed a 'little protest group'. Ramsey asked, 'Who's that over there?' In response, Ramsey admitted, the mayor 'was a little dismissive', explaining: 'I'll tell you who doesn't like this program. It's the drug dealers.' Ramsey continued sarcastically, 'What a worry!'[21] Of course, when those surveyed stated the card was making their lives better, this was also taken to indicate the card was working.

I see it differently. I offer this not as a whole explanation but an observation arrived at over time, which explains why some people were more likely to object to the card whereas others were more positive or just benign about it. In my experience, the most articulate and passionate critics of the card were far from narrowly thinking of themselves and their own frustrated desires. In fact, they were often those attuned to broader colonial, racial and social injustices. They sought to understand the card from a historical and political perspective. Conversations with these community members were far-ranging, encompassing discussion of terra nullius; over-policing; the Intervention; the dismantling of CDEP and the capricious administration of its replacement, CDP … among other topics. Those people I spent time with who liked the card were less interested in those larger issues, leaving them in the background. More immediate, familial concerns were foregrounded and claimed their attention.

∴

Aero and I settled on to a threadbare couch. Seated beside him, I pressed record: 'Take me back to where it begins, Aero.'

'It begins,' he said, when he was about 12 or 13. 'I sort of was on the streets. I had family but I was still on the street. I was streetwise. I could get anything I wanted on the street.' This was in a place I'll call Somersby, which 'used to be the second most feared place in Australia'. Aero describes it: 'It's got all industrial there. Like, BP refinery, Alcoa and BHP was there. A lot of us worked down there.' Aero also worked on farms, from when he was 13.

'Went down to the farms until about 17 and then come back into town and then started working on the shutdown. So, we were on good money.' After his time on the maintenance shutdowns, Aero worked on the lines. His dad was a linesman, working for the state electricity company.

'So, I become a linesman and I worked there for about five years until a bloke died on me.' Aero's workmate was electrocuted. 'He was on another pole to me. I had to run down my pole and run up to get him off. I gave him mouth-to-mouth for half an hour and he was dead.' Aero gave it away after this. 'Every time I went up the pole, I could see him.'

Before Aero's dad was a linesman, he was a showman. And Aero, too, 'worked on a sideshow meself for a while'. This 'was a good experience because you got around the countryside and you met a lot of people'. It was a 'rugged life'. Free tickets for girls upset their boyfriends.

Aero's dad had tattoos from his carny days. 'I got my first one when I was 13.' Soon enough, he had 'love' and 'hate' printed across his knuckles. There was nothing else to do in boys' homes. 'I done all these on meself, on the legs.' Aero shifted around Australia, driving trucks. 'I always find me own job. Either truck driving or digging holes. In them days you could get them sort of jobs.'

Pointing to the tats, I asked, 'Are the drawings, like, meaningful, Aero?' 'Not really.'

Aero was 18, maybe 19, when he got his first sentence: six months for vagrancy. Hitching from Melbourne to Sydney, he was picked up in Wangaratta. 'Because I didn't have any means of support, so they reckon. Called me a rogue and a vagabond, me and my mate.' A few years ago, he went back for a short stint. 'The kids all called me "Pop".'

When Aero first went to jail, it was like a brotherhood. 'When you get out of jail, people only talk to ya because they're scared of ya. It's just hard to blend back in.' He insists, 'We had ethics. You could leave your cell open and no one would steal.' In jail, he drank potato brew. One Christmas, he drank boot stiffener. 'We had our own way of doing things; don't you worry.' Aero served a pretty long sentence and became the prison barber. 'I can cut hair; don't you worry about that.' He cut the officers' hair and trafficked goods in his barber's kit.

Aero clashed with his dad, the linesman, the showman. 'I seem to have lost them all in one year. They went bang, bang, bang. Lost me parents, me nan, the whole lot in one year. I lost the lot. And that didn't go down well.'

Aero could have told me all sorts of things. He could have told me about the Somersby motorbike gang but … 'better not'. Aero showed me how to scrub the teacups thoroughly in the community centre's kitchen. He saw me coming, no doubt, with my cutesy tattoos. It turns out Aero has one meaningful tattoo, after all. His 'missus'.

The card was making him depressed. 'I want to send money to me wife every now and then.' A social worker got involved. Aero was able to get off the card by securing an exemption under what was known as the 'wellbeing exemption'. That is, if 'being a Cashless Debit Card program participant would seriously risk that person's mental, physical or emotional wellbeing', there existed provisions for the Secretary of the Department of Social Service to exempt them from participating in the program.[22]

Aero's stories kept coming. He paid a friend 200 bucks to borrow their car and drive it across the Nullarbor. Four kangaroos jumped out at the car one early morning, causing him to hide the $1400 he'd recently won in the Lotto, in case his friend insisted he pay for the repairs. He planned to go to the wreckers, do them himself, 'piece of piss'.

And you know what? He was only one number off winning a million.

∴

In prison, Aero drank boot stiffener. As he says above, 'We had our own ways of doing things.' In Ceduna, people found their own ways of getting around the card.

'I guess it's like anything. There's always a way around it,' it was explained to me. How? 'Like, "Hey, I'll fill up your car and give [me] $80 cash" and, you know, "You use my card and put $150 fuel on it."' Another young person, living in a household of heavy drinkers, shook his head ruefully, unhappily, in response to me asking whether people could get around the card. 'Drunks gonna drink!'

'Yeah, the card is no good,' I was told. 'And it doesn't work, it just doesn't work because people, they find many ways of getting the money around and getting the cash in hand.' Also, 'And all come together, you know, and chuck in a little bit here, little bit there ...' And, 'The thing about it is people who are elderly and exempt from being on the card they're vulnerable targets of assaults.' And, 'Only recently, like a couple of months ago, a lady had her arm broken [by] her own son ... To support their habit, like. It's ridiculous.'

The incident mentioned above was not the only story relayed to me of a senior Aboriginal person being assaulted in an effort to gain access to cash. Yet this was a rationale for the card's introduction: its potential to protect caregivers from the constant demands to share cash, which in turn affected their ability to spend their incomes on the children they are responsible for.[23]

'You reckon people can get around the card?' I asked June.

'Of course, they can! They think blackfellas is stupid. Blackfellas not stupid ... They walk around like they don't know nothing, but they smart. They know to use their brain.'

Another person depicted the main street as a scene of hustle. 'You go down the street, there, you got everybody, all looking around. [They are thinking:] "How I'm gonna get money, how am I going to try for this card? Who's card can I put it in?" They're thinking down the street, those people that got paid today, "Who's got that money in the card?" They're thinking really hard, "How am I going to get this money in my hand? Because I can't get anything with the card but, like what I really, really want ..."'

More concretely, someone explained to me, 'What they'll do is they'll go buy a laptop on the card and then flog the laptop.'

'For cheap?' I clarified.

They replied, 'Yep. Cheaper, yeah. Well, they buy radio or they buy a telephone. What do ya call the ...? An iPhone and then they'll flog the iPhone for less, to get money to go to grog.'

I then asked, 'Have you seen people do that?'

They replied, 'Yes, I have. And I don't ... You can't blame the people that are ... you know. It's against the rights, human rights, because they should be able to do what they like with their money. The government's saying they can't and they're making the decisions like they did years ago when they took the Stolen Generation away. They're making the decisions, which is not fair. Not fair.'

Another of my interviewees admitted, 'I have bought large-ticket items on my card, received the cash for it. I did it twice ... And I think if you're in a position where you can saddle up with someone who's got some kind of ready income and who's able to do little things like that, well and good.'

I also interviewed a community worker who told me he had observed both 'lots of swapping cards' and 'conflict' surrounding these transactions. For example, he talked of promises of reimbursement on Indue cards and people then being handed Indue cards that were 'empty'. He saw these as essentially similar 'tensions' to those that surrounded the sharing of cash.

Elena, whose life was enmeshed with her non-Aboriginal, Greek and Aboriginal kin, shared her experience: 'Of course they can [buy alcohol], yeah … People chuck in, drink their life away … What they needed to build here was a rehab centre for people to actually go in, not send 'em away to be away from their families. I know from my ex-partner: he was sent away for rehab. He was missing his family, got out and went back on heavy drugs. If there was a rehab centre here, instead of a Hungry Jacks, he could have probably … put his mind to it. Could have done daily visits or something. That's one thing they need to think about.' The nearest residential drug and alcohol rehabilitation facility is located in Port Augusta, almost 500 kilometres west of Ceduna.

Elena had her own reasons and strategies for getting access to cash. Excited and apprehensive about an upcoming holiday, she fretted about the card potentially not working on the east coast. 'If it doesn't work, I'm stuck!' So she sold make-up and other sundry items in her personal possession 'as cheap as it can go', through a local Facebook group.

Finally, an especially puissant Aboriginal man told me carefully, 'They're trying to stop people from drinking. When they made this stuff.' He reflected with poignancy on the introduction of alcohol and drugs—'this stuff'—as part of the colonisation process. 'They made the alcohol. And it never stops. You can't stop people from drinking.' He told me despairingly, 'We've lost our vision. A card cannot give vision to the community.'

••

'Is the cashless debit card working?' This was the title of an ABC TV *7.30* segment dedicated to the card's rollout in Queensland. The reporter explained that there, in the fourth trial site, the target was youth unemployment: the card was issued to welfare recipients aged 35 and younger. As to whether it was working or not, the evidence, the viewer was told, was 'inconclusive' and largely 'anecdotal' to boot: equally passionate supporters and detractors were interviewed.[24]

'Is it working?' was never my question. I asked instead, 'Tell me about your life.' I also asked, 'What's it like to be on the card?' My work is about exploring the lives and stories of those affected by the card through their own words, rather than on policy-makers' terms. However, other researchers, both academic and applied, have tackled this question in greater depth and nuance than a journalist is granted.

As mentioned earlier, ORIMA Research was contracted to produce a report evaluating the card's performance during its first twelve months. The trial of the card was found to have had a 'considerable positive impact'.[25] However, the shortcomings of this contracted research have been highlighted by numerous experts, who point out that it relied largely on self-reported behaviour change, which might well be influenced by an interviewee's reluctance to disclose that they engage in drinking or, especially, illicit drug use.[26] In July 2018, the Australian National Audit Office released a damning report analysing the implementation and performance of the cashless debit card trial. Focusing on the paucity of baseline data available to and analysed by ORIMA, among other issues, the Audit Office report stated that it was difficult to ascertain 'whether there had been a reduction in social harm' as a result of the card's introduction.[27]

Another interesting analysis was offered by a team of researchers who combed over store sales data and who used public intoxication as a proxy for alcohol sales data, which is not available. These researchers concluded that there was 'little evidence' that the card has 'affected targeted behaviours'.[28] They did observe an increase in spending on food but also a rise in the proportion of sales of energy-dense, nutrient-poor discretionary foods.

Another team of academic researchers used both surveys and interviews to uncover, overwhelmingly, 'negative experiences' of income management. Their important work documents 'feelings of stigma, shame and frustration that result from being caught up in a set of policies that are perceived as unnecessary, unhelpful and/or harmful'.[29] Shame is also a topic of importance to me and is explored more fully in chapter 6.

Finally, a long-delayed second evaluation, undertaken by a team of researchers at the University of Adelaide, was somewhat inconclusive. Examining the first three trial sites of Ceduna, the East Kimberley and the Goldfields, the authors found 'consistent and clear evidence' for a reduction in alcohol consumption, but also stated that this finding could not be attributed solely to the card.[30] A million dollars of extra federal government funding, for example, was committed to Ceduna when the card was first introduced. This funding provided for a range of initiatives, including a mobile team to patrol the streets and connect vulnerable people with social services.[31] This more supportive and holistic initiative, among others, might explain the reduction in drinking that the evaluation found.

My interview with Pam gives some clue to as why the efficacy or otherwise of the card still seemed so unclear five years after its introduction. What would 'success' even look like? Pam said to me, 'I think the biggest issue with the card was that realistically the government hadn't done their baseline data correctly. And they actually hadn't decided what datasets they were gonna chase to prove that this card was worth anything. And by the time they thought about that, the horse had well and truly bolted.' Put more directly, 'You still have not got what it is you're trying to achieve clearly articulated and ways to measure it. That is the biggest problem.'

••

How does this story end, then? Unimpressed with the inconclusiveness of the two commissioned evaluations undertaken into the card and persuaded by arguments regarding its ideological character, the Labor Party went to the 2022 election promising to scrap the cashless debit card. The proverbial nail in the coffin for the card seemed to come in the early days of the Albanese government. The Australian National Audit Office released a second, follow-up report into the implementation and performance of the cashless debit card. This time, the Audit Office highlighted that the second evaluation did not overcome the problems that plagued the first. Indeed, it could not: there 'was no baseline data collected or used for any of the regions prior to implementation of the [card's trial] to assist with establishing program impact'.[32] So Pam was right about that.

Further, the second evaluation had been delayed by eighteen months, and there was limited evidence that it informed parliament's decision to extend the use of the card, which was made in December 2020 and before this second evaluation was publicly available.[33] In other words, the

Morrison government argued for the card's extension without drawing on credible and publicly available evidence that it served the positive social role they believed it did.

In response to the release of the second Audit Office report, the new Minister for Social Services, Amanda Rishworth, assured media that she had already instructed her department 'to prepare for its termination'.[34] In September 2022, legislation passed both houses of parliament providing for people on the cashless debit card in Ceduna, the East Kimberley, the Goldfields and in Bundaberg–Hervey Bay in Queensland to transition off the card.[35] The process was simple: one phone call to Services Australia was all it took to get off the card. Cardholders in these four localities may choose to still have their income managed. If they so elect, the plan is for their income to be managed via a new card administered by Services Australia.

It is a different story for those on the cashless debit card in the Northern Territory and Cape York. Recall that these cardholders switched from the BasicsCard to the cashless debit card as per the Morrison government's 2020 legislation. In these localities, cashless debit cardholders will remain subject to income management. This will also eventually be facilitated via the new card administered by Services Australia.[36] Compulsory income management remains in the Northern Territory, for now. The cashless debit card has been abolished.

5

'Why are you crying? We're here to help you'

For the first two months of Svetlana's daughter's life, the pair couch-surfed and lived on the streets. Granted public housing, Svetlana then worked to 'stabilise' herself and slowly form 'new ties'. A 'former addict', she had been 'clean and sober for six years'. Her daughter faced speech delays, and with help from a social service, Svetlana had been focused on supporting her, deciding to keep her at pre-school for an additional year. Svetlana's father, who has dementia, had lately moved to an aged care facility, leaving her mother 'all alone' and 'very sick'.

'On top of all this, ParentsNext was introduced to me,' she told me. 'I wanted to keep an open mind,' she continued, 'and I did.' The official description of ParentsNext is that it 'helps parents with children under six, to plan and prepare for future study or employment'.[1] Paid work is Svetlana's aspiration, and after a long break since her role as an administrator in a corporate setting, she was 'terrified'. ParentsNext seemed to promise a bridge between the past and future.

'The phantom phone call' was how Svetlana referred to it. She remembered receiving an alert: 'We'll call you at this time. And if you don't answer, your payments might be suspended.' The phone call didn't arrive at the specified time; her 'heart was missing a beat'. Then, at the day's close, the phone call came, confirming her eligibility for ParentsNext. She was 'happy to get help'.

Svetlana repeated, simply and without shame, 'I need help.'

In early December 2018, she went to a meeting with her ParentsNext case manager and was 'bamboozled' with information about where to report, when to report, how to report. Svetlana continued to report to Centrelink, as per the conditions of Parenting Payment (Single). She did not realise she had agreed to an additional layer of reporting requirements via a different app; on 24 December, her payment was suspended.

To be clear, 'it wasn't like they completely fucked me over'. She 'battened down the hatches', and Christmas went ahead. It was more that she was 'in tears' and there was her four-year-old and Svetlana having to 'pretend that everything was OK'. That was what made the Christmas of 2018 'so hard'.

By the time Svetlana's ParentsNext provider reopened in the new year, she had a new case manager. 'That lady', who had seemed 'overworked, jaded and cynical'—the one who explained verbally that ParentsNext essentially involved mastering a second reporting system—was gone. Her replacement 'apologised profusely', and together they set to work on a participation plan. Svetlana suggested that her weekly participation activity be, in effect, caring.

When they arrived in Australia from Ukraine, Svetlana's parents moved into public housing in an inner-city tower. They left behind a 'good life' but sought a better one. They didn't 'speak a word of English'; Svetlana started at a local school and excelled, learning English quickly. She became her parents' interpreter.

'I was lonely,' Svetlana reflected. Migration involved leaving behind an extended family, and her parents were fearful of their surrounds: the estate was 'rough', 'dirty' and 'dangerous'. 'I know my dad carried a kitchen knife with, like, a proper blade with him, whenever he went out.'

Svetlana achieved admission to one of Sydney's academically prestigious selective schools but felt sorely out of place. She started truanting, ran away from home, slept on the streets. Later, she escaped the streets by forming a relationship with a violent boyfriend. Meanwhile, she went to TAFE and worked a range of 'boring' jobs: as a PA, for example, she filled out someone else's diary—it was 'soul destroying'. She cycled in and out of rehab and addiction, determinedly clawing her way out of the dangerous relationship.

Becoming a parent, with a later boyfriend, she was 'terrified of losing my child'. It proved the final impetus to stay clean, move to a new area and carefully begin to let new people into her life, avoiding 'any hint' of drug use. 'I had to just keep this baby alive, you know, and myself.'

So, did it count, she asked her empathetic new case manager, that she looked after her little girl and also caught two buses across the city each way, each day, to visit her lonely, ailing mum? Was caring for others a legitimate 'activity'?

'That's not in our abilities to put it in as an activity,' came the response. As 'helpful' as she tried to be, Svetlana's new case manager—'freshly graduated', 'idealistic', 'you can tell it's getting a bit much'—still seemed intent on 'ticking boxes'.

They agreed, instead, that Svetlana would enrol in a TAFE course that would qualify her to seek work as a receptionist in a medical centre. Yet Svetlana discovered she had become so 'unplugged from the system' that self-directed, online study was far more daunting than she envisaged. She floundered. The fragility of her confidence was painfully evident to me.

A sudden health emergency, three weeks before our interview, turned into a 'real saga' and had interrupted her efforts at study. She had secured a temporary exemption from ParentsNext. 'It gives me up until Christmas,' she explained. 'So, again, I find myself …'

The thought trailed off. Soon after, I prompted quietly, 'Should we leave it there?'

'Yes, please.'

••

Svetlana called it the 'phantom phone call'. Other interviewees shared their experience of receiving variously confusing, nerve-wracking and initially welcome phone calls to discuss ParentsNext.

Anna recalled an email alerting her to a phone call she was soon to receive, also to assess her eligibility. She was sent a follow-up text message confirming the time and date of the phone call. The call itself was never made; 'they never actually rang'. Her payment was immediately suspended because of a 'failure to attend' what was in effect a compulsory appointment.

In Eloise's case, 'I got a phone call out of the blue from, um—I don't know which agency it was ...'

The caller said, 'I need to ask you some questions about a new thing we're doing. It's called ParentsNext.'

Eloise responded: 'And I was like, "OK" ... I had no idea who they were. I didn't know what they were talking about.'

Lefa's caller was 'this really lovely gentleman'. She imitated a sales pitch. 'It was kind of like, "You've been selected!!"' Working their way through the questions that determine eligibility, he 'genuinely seemed to be asking questions about how I am and where I'm at with my life and my studies'.

Ayesha told me, 'I got a short letter, sort of pointing ... towards, oh, they want to help me get back into the workforce. And so there will be training and this and that.' Ayesha said to herself, 'Yes, please.' This letter pre-empted the call undertaken to determine her eligibility for the program. Unlike Svetlana's and Anna's, Ayesha's phone call was made at the specified time.

'The call that I got, Eve, was very far away.' Far away, that is, from the structured support she understood and hoped the letter referred to. 'So, there was no talk of training as such.' Further, 'I'm trying to put this in the most ... generous way as I can. But the person who rung me was maybe an 18-year-old with not a lot of life experience. Um, and someone who's probably doing this as a casual job.' Indeed, Ayesha's caller was likely a low-wage worker employed by multinational conglomerate Serco, which holds the contract to run Centrelink call centres and Australia's onshore refugee detention centres, among a host of other interests.[2]

Ayesha's eligibility assessment interview proceeded. 'She didn't understand what my degree was. I've got two master's degrees, and she didn't understand the concept of what a master's degree is.' Ayesha grew up in Kolkata and was educated in the United Kingdom before migrating to Australia.

Ayesha's young caller kept repeating, 'So have you completed school?' After about '15, 20 minutes' of Ayesha's explanations meeting incomprehension, she said simply, 'Yes, I have completed school.' Ayesha next explained that she had been working within workplace health and safety. 'So, then she said, "OK, so can [you] start working as a labourer?"'

Ayesha was getting nowhere. Her caller homed in on 'either bricklaying or getting into labour work'. Her daughter 'was waiting for her next feed'. Ayesha said, 'That's fine. Just put me onto whatever program you have to.'

∴

The protagonist of satirical novella *Simpson Returns* is legendary ANZAC stretcher-bearer John Simpson Kirkpatrick, who carried wounded soldiers at Gallipoli on a donkey to the beach to await evacuation. In *Simpson Returns*, man and ass are 'eighty-eight years resurrected' and searching for the inland sea. Their epic, ill-fated journey proceeds by way of a series of encounters with archetypical figures of contemporary Australian disadvantage. Simpson and his donkey Murphy are not visible to all. They represent 'Old Truth, Enduring Myth, Simple Hope, Unfashionable Kindness'. Those who need to see them, see them.[3] Tellingly, the first character who sees them—who needs them—is a single mother in her late thirties. This fictional single mum has three kids to support and a household to run, and has become embroiled in an expensive and draining legal dispute about the child support moneys owed to her.

According to the 2021 Census, 15 per cent of Australian families are 'one-parent families'. The 'vast majority' of one-parent families with children and dependants are single-mother families—approximately 82 per cent.[4] Single-parent families are exposed to poverty for many reasons: their reliance on one income; lower levels of employment because of caring responsibilities and inadequate access to childcare; and because of the low welfare payment rate for sole parents, who are then moved onto the even lower JobSeeker rate when their youngest child turns eight.[5]

My single-mum interviewees were matter of fact about their poverty. Ciara was automatically enrolled in group sessions when she began ParentsNext. When the group was offered advice about budgeting, she retorted: 'Honey, single mothers are one of the most budget extreme people you can come across. Like, we know how to budget!'

••

If the BasicsCard was the precursor to the cashless debit card, then ParentsNext's precursor was the 2006 Welfare to Work policy. 'Welfare to Work represented a radical change in policies affecting Australian single parents,' explains sociologist Michelle Brady.[6] Simone Casey elaborates, noting that previously parenting itself was treated as a 'legitimate social role', with minimal conditions attached to the income support available to impoverished parents. Under the Welfare to Work changes, sole parents were essentially 'reclassified' as unemployed from when their youngest child turned eight.[7]

Brady conducted research with frontline staff implementing Welfare to Work. She shows that some case managers continued to foreground their clients' 'identities as mothers', attempting to facilitate 'employment that fitted into school hours'.[8] Other private outfits implemented the same policy differently, treating their clients as job seekers and erasing their care work and commitments. Casey talked with single mothers affected by the 'shock' of being reclassified from the role of mother to being unemployed. 'It was as if,' one mum described, 'someone had waved a magic wand and the value of parenting had changed overnight.'[9] Casey's interviewees rued the compromised care of their children: some expressed that their children were left unsupervised after school while they worked.

ParentsNext waves the wand again. As Trish, a single mum, pointed out, 'normally you don't start getting harassed by Centrelink until your kid's about to go to school or something like that'. For Trish, ParentsNext brings forward harassment's start date.

I agree with Trish but formulate it in more technical terms: the significance of ParentsNext is that it represents an extension of welfare conditions to circumstances previously protected from them. ParentsNext reclassifies the parents of very young children—initially six-month-old babies and now nine-month-old babies—as 'workers in waiting', who need to partake in monitored activities.[10] Yet their designation is different from and their treatment more ambiguous than that of 'the unemployed'.

To recap: ParentsNext participants are required to engage in one of a range of possible activities, and some of these are certainly tied to and compatible with parenting. Attending playgroup and story time sessions at local libraries 'count' as legitimate activities. When I interviewed Shelby, she told me that her son was already attending movement classes at her own expense and that this was accepted as her weekly activity. Shelby, a domestic abuse survivor and fully qualified nurse, had to report online that she was taking her son to a weekly event she had already enrolled him in and paid for and that he enjoys. This does little to better prepare her to restart her career once he starts school, which is her hope. However, the reporting requirement acculturates her to social security with conditions and to digitally surveilled compliance.

Other approved ParentsNext activities more obviously direct participants towards employment. Volunteering, engaging in study and searching for jobs are other acceptable activities.

ParentsNext first operated in ten disadvantaged locations in 2016. When it was rolled out nationally, these disadvantaged localities were flagged as 'intensive streams', and a further twenty localities were also designated 'intensive'. Those additional twenty were selected because of the high proportion of Aboriginal and Torres Strait Islander recipients of Parenting Payment in those areas.[11] An explicit aim of ParentsNext is to 'close the gap' in Aboriginal and Torres Strait Islander people's employment outcomes.[12] This 'intensive' designation meant there were at this time two different kinds of participants in ParentsNext: those in the thirty intensive streams came with participation funding, which could potentially be spent to facilitate them partaking in activities; participants living outside those localities did not.

In 2021, these two streams were merged. All participants now have a $1200 fund attached to them, although this is disbursed to the provider and is not designated to be spent on a specific individual.[13] Aboriginal and Torres Strait Islander people continue to be over-represented within ParentsNext: they comprised 21 per cent of the ParentsNext caseload as of May 2021. Further, figures from late 2018 show that at that stage Aboriginal and Torres Strait Islander parents comprised 19 per cent of participants and were subject to 24 per cent of the payment suspensions.[14]

As well as increased access to the Participation Fund, the eligibility criteria for ParentsNext has been revised. In 2018, parents could be deemed eligible for compulsory enrolment in ParentsNext when their babies were just six months old; that is, this welfare measure suggested that with a six-month-old to tend to, one's future employment prospects and goals need to come into focus. My memory of the six-month, sleep-deprived mark is this: I read somewhere that it was time to start thinking about introducing solid food, which I duly did. It was flung around the room before my baby wailed for the breast. My focus, in other words, was my baby, even if there was more to my life than parenting. Under pressure to accept that six-month-old babies are still unpredictable and demanding, eligibility for mandatory participation in ParentsNext was changed to nine months in mid-2021. One further tweak to ParentsNext is important to note. In late 2020 the automatic and immediate suspension of payments was replaced with a two-day grace period.[15]

••

In Ceduna, I hung around. The cashless debit card was a welfare reform initiative anchored in particular places, and my efforts to understand people's experience of it were in situ. My research into ParentsNext proceeded differently.

I circulated a call for interviewees on social media. Slowly, often cautiously, women contacted me wanting to talk. Anxiety pervaded many of these exchanges; reassurances about anonymity were sought. One person, Misha, created a new email account for the purpose of corresponding with me, so concerned was she that her ParentsNext provider might find out she was criticising the program: 'They will go after you if your name becomes public.'

I recorded that life story interview with Svetlana in her flat in a public housing walk-up, the door to a balcony thrown open to the sunshine and trilling lorikeets. My Little Ponies with tangled fluorescent hair and baskets of clean washing were perched on the couch. I interviewed Eloise in a beautiful new rental on Sydney's bushy edges, which she shared with her son and friends; until three weeks previously she had lived alone with her pre-school-aged child in a 'very, very small granny flat that flooded'. I met up with Natasha in a comfortable, carpeted club, and we sipped cappuccinos.

Interviews with women in their homes and in places of their choosing were longer than the interviews I conducted by phone. A recording device, the late Janet Malcolm reflected, preserves the words that pass between interviewer and interviewee but cannot 'catch any of the language of face and body by which we all speak to one another and sometimes say what we dare not put into words'.[16] Interviewing women over the phone made it harder to sense—let alone capture—this other exchange. Yet, perhaps especially because so much communication now takes place via the written word, phone calls are also strangely intimate as both parties strain towards each other, listening intently and carefully deciding to fill, tolerate or probe the lulls that occur at intervals. A layer of apprehending another—of making something of a person's face, their style, their bodily being—is stripped away: there are only two voices and the static.

Talking over the phone also freed my interviewees to attend to other tasks: I could often hear them moving around—picking up toys, I imagined, or putting away dishes and making asides to small children. 'Oh, it's all right, darlin',' Anna soothed her youngest. Anna is a single mother of three boys and described a 'high-energy household'. When I interviewed her, she was working casual shifts with people affected by a spinal cord injury. Anna was relatively new to ParentsNext and, despite having her payment suspended after that first phone call never transpired, she 'didn't have a lot of negative to say about it, to be honest'.

··

Anna wasn't the only one of my interviewees whose criticism of ParentsNext was muted. This is not to say these interviewees valued or defended the program in its current form. They saw themselves as dragooned to take part in something that primarily inconvenienced them; an arbitrary ask to be swatted away so that they could return their focus to the reality of their lives and more high-stakes claims on them: the needs of their children and others in their life; their own efforts to shape their present and future.

Lauris was 'already thinking of attending a playgroup anyway, so it was quite easy for me to come up with something' for her participation plan. The online reporting system was 'easy to use': Lauris set reminders in her phone to ensure she didn't forget. There was that time she received a text saying her payment was about to be suspended, but that was straightforward to sort out. Overall, then, what did she make of ParentsNext? 'I think it is a complete waste of my time.'

Lauris had been working in admin roles continuously since leaving school early. She planned on finding a job that fitted in with her two kids' school days: 'I'm not looking for a career, just a job I can do.' It was important to her to raise her children instead of having childcare workers spend time with them. But when the moment comes, 'I know how to write a great résumé, prepare for a job interview, dress for an interview, know how to look online and apply for jobs.' Lauris's calm and confidence contrasted with her evocation of the nearest agency contracted to provide ParentsNext.

Lauris had seen six separate case workers and had to explain her circumstances repeatedly. While she appreciated that her provider had never been 'pushy', they were also alarmingly disorganised. She had filled out 'exactly' the same survey twice and was once booked in for two separate appointments on the same day. While on the face of it this chaos looks like an indictment of this provider—and it is—the sociologist Lisa Adkins also makes an important point about conditional welfare states, which 'command' recipients to 'constantly adapt to unpredictability'. This command, Adkins argues, is continuous with the world of low-wage, unpredictable and casualised work, for which these recipients are being prepared and frequently already engage in.[17] To return to Lauris's circumstances: every time she had a ParentsNext appointment, her own mum took time off work to drive her there.

Kylie was also much less critical and voluble in our conversation about her experiences than others motivated to speak with me. A single mother with a baby girl, she articulated a strong goal: she was studying at a regional university to become an 'Indigenous midwife'; she told me she hoped to be part of addressing the gap between Aboriginal and non-Aboriginal maternal health. Kylie briskly summed up that ParentsNext involved speaking to 'useless people', dealing with a 'broken system' and travelling 100 kilometres each way to attend an appointment every three months. 'Many times, I have arrived and my caseworker went home early or didn't go to work that day without calling me or cancelling.'

Eloise also complained about the hassle of travelling two hours by train to attend a 5–10-minute appointment and then waiting half an hour for her return train. She had done this trip every three months for a year before a new case manager switched her appointments to phone calls. For Eloise, however, the costs of participation in the program seemed less contained than they were for Anna, Lauris and Kylie.

••

I met Eloise in a house set deep in thick, tinder-dry bush. We ate strawberries while a fierce morning heat steadily swelled to fill the kitchen and a high, milky white sky. Within weeks of us meeting, the east coast was ablaze.

Eloise was in pain. A long search for a diagnosis had recently led to the conclusion that she has Ehlers–Danlos syndrome, which affects connective tissue. In other words, she was 'too sick to work and not sick enough' for the Disability Support Pension.

When Eloise got that first phone call about ParentsNext, 'out of the blue', she was just 'trying to work out what I was going to do with my health'. The caller asked a series of questions about educational attainment and her son's age. She then scheduled an appointment for Eloise for the next day, in an outer Sydney suburb that was a two-hour train ride away. 'I don't have a car. I have a toddler and a chronic illness. Like, I don't know what you expect me to do.

'I remember very vividly her saying, "Why are you crying? We're here to help you; we're trying to help you."' Eloise continued, 'I've been dealing with them ever since.'

Eloise signed a participation plan, agreeing to go to TAFE to complete her Higher School Certificate. 'I wanted to do it anyway,' she reasoned. 'In retrospect, I would've picked something else so I could go to TAFE without stress and do it at my own pace and not with payments-getting-cut hanging over my head.'

Eloise left school in Year 9 but completed Year 10 at TAFE and remained grateful for the support and understanding she received from TAFE teachers. 'I was the prodigy that never went anywhere,' she told me. 'Very good marks until …' A severe eating disorder. Suicide attempts. Plural. 'Also, being visibly brown in a very white school did not help.' For Eloise's single mum, 'education was the ticket out of poverty'. Her mum had slowly completed a degree and was now working as a counsellor. The two of them were meant to show the world that 'We can do just as good as you can'.

At 21, Eloise became a mum. Like her own mother, she was acutely conscious of others' judgements: 'dumb girls have babies'.

The Ehlers–Danlos diagnosis solved some problems but threw up new ones. 'I am not sure how to toe the line between, "Yes, I'm too disabled to get a job, but I am not too disabled to look after my son."'

'Looking after him is my priority and has been my life for four years … I love being a mum!'

Me: 'What do you love about it?'

Eloise: 'Oh, he's cool. My kid's just cool! He's really funny … I like hearing the weird stuff he comes out with.' We talked of his pre-schooling, watching him relate to friends, his growing relationship with his dad— they play video games together. 'I like watching him understand concepts, like watching him start to get the hang of what I'm trying to pass on to him.'

Parenting, Eloise reflected, is 'the first thing I've ever felt that I was kind of good at'.

••

'Useless people' was Kylie's summing up of her interactions with ParentsNext providers. Who are these people? Michelle Brady explains that what she calls 'personalized planning programs' are to 'contemporary welfare systems in the United States, the United Kingdom, Canada and Australia what subsidized training and public employment programs were to the post-war welfare state'. That is, access to income support in the contemporary welfare state is conditional on the development of and adherence to an individualised agreement that emerges via 'one-on-one meetings with individual advisers'.[18] I recorded a lot of material on the topic of interactions with these individual advisers, variously called case managers, caseworkers, 'the provider', 'the lady there', 'the new girl', 'my worker', 'the woman that I spoke to', 'my support person'.

An enlightening recent study introduces the reader to 'employment consultants' previously employed as hairdressers, in hospitality and as flight attendants.[19] They are part of a volatile and highly feminised low-paid workforce that has been markedly deskilled and deunionised since welfare delivery was privatised and subject to tender processes, and the emphasis has shifted to enforcing conditions.[20]

Some frontline workers certainly perceive that empathetic listening and attention is at least the one thing they do have in their arsenal to give their clients, since to assist them to find work when there is not enough work to go around is not within their power.[21] Others go above and beyond to broker work and training opportunities where they do exist. Interactions with frontline workers, according to a different study, might also be shaped by race—aggressive white clients can leverage their race privilege to assert their rights and attempt to intimidate workers from non-white backgrounds; in turn, these workers might identify with and feel especially supportive towards migrants and refugees whose circumstances are familiar to them.[22]

A consistent theme in research into this system is that the coercive work case managers do, in emphasising and enforcing compliance through computerised systems, is more keenly felt and perceived than the supportive work they do. Further, those working these roles in the conditional, privatised welfare system increasingly view their 'clients' negatively, seeing them as individually responsible for their circumstances.[23] Below are some of the stories I collected about these interactions.

'One of them told me to dye my hair blonde and get blue contacts … One of them refuted the information that my doctor provided. I handed them the document, "This is what my specialist said …", but they said, "No, speak to your doctor again." It was like they had more power than the doctor.'

'When I got help preparing my résumé, there were lots of errors. Even my phone number was incorrect.'

'The lady there knew what my circumstances were and that I'm actively looking for work. Um, so she's helped me out. I had to stop work about five years ago just to raise [my daughter] … [S]he asked very thorough questions; it wasn't sort of pointing me towards doing something that I haven't done. Then she also helped me with, um, getting a cover letter ready, sort of base cover letter, which I sort of change towards whatever the job requirements are. So, it's sort of been a silver lining, having her part of this process. Because, yeah, she's quite empathetic. She understands.'

Māori foster mother Jo relayed, 'So I met her. Her name is [Belinda]. My worker. She got surprised with me that I knew a lot. She liked my questions.' Belinda began to explain to Jo that ParentsNext 'is a new government program and … this is how they going to roll it out for …' Jo 'interjected her': 'I was actually telling her that foster carers are exempt from these types of programs and her reply was, "I don't know that; I need to find out for myself."' Jo, in other words, knew more about the program than the worker tasked with enforcing its conditions.[24]

'I'm really exhausted. I'm broke,' summed up Misha. Also: 'I really want work for the income. I was going to the providers for help and they're making mistakes with my resume. Some of them were like, "You don't need to come in." They would dismiss me.'

While Svetlana perceived that her new, more supportive case manager was a recent university graduate, others sensed that case managers might well have themselves been 'sort of quite downtrodden by the system and then now they're suddenly in this semi-sales position'. In these cases, when people have 'been at the bottom' themselves, there can exist an almost evangelical edge: 'I'm going to help people and I'm, yeah, a little bit better than these people because I've worked hard and I deserve it.'

Ella, introduced in chapter 1, told her case manager that she had mistakenly been found eligible for ParentsNext and had then been deemed ineligible. The case manager replied with, 'Oh? I think someone's telling porky pies.' Ella's reaction: 'And I'm like, what the fuck? And then, um, I said, yeah. I said, "Look, lady, I'm not eligible."' Ella affected the case manager's dripping, syrupy voice. *Porky pies.* 'That tone you're adopting,' I said. 'It's …' Ella jumped in: 'Patronising. Disgusting.'

∴

Lallie described to me her first encounter with Australia's welfare system: 'Oh, my God, you have a system?! That looks after you? Geee! I came from war. There is no back-up. There was just early insecurity: physical, emotional, psychological insecurity.' Lallie and her family are African refugees who settled in Brisbane when she was 10. Medicare, too, was a revelation.

Lallie completed high school in Brisbane and then went to university. Even before graduating, a path stretched before her. After gaining her degree, she worked in community sector roles in homeless services, sexual health and mental health. She also designed, launched and began running a consultancy on the side.

Her consultancy was just beginning to take off when COVID-19 hit. No more 'toxic workplaces'; no more 'working with dickheads'. And, most importantly, she could devote more time to her youngest child, who had just been diagnosed with a complex medical condition. 'I have to stay close to home, I have to be here more.' She needed room to breathe. Without a regular income, Lallie found herself on Parenting Payment (Single) and then on ParentsNext.

I interviewed Lallie over the phone. She was articulate, compelling, forceful. I had no trouble imagining her first appointment with her ParentsNext case manager, which also took place over the phone. Lallie told her: 'This is where I'm at in life. My child has these needs.' Lallie insisted that taking her child to appointments be counted as her 'participation activity' rather than doing something new. The case manager checked with her supervising manager and then acquiesced.

This was Lallie's approach: 'How do I make this work for me, immediately?' She emphasised, 'How do I make this work for me? Because I don't have time for bullshit. I just don't have time for Centrelink to be dangling me left and right.' Impressed with Lallie's plans for her consultancy, her case manager next agreed to upgrade Lallie's Zoom account and to buy lights so that Lallie's work could successfully transition online. Soon, Lallie was back at work, 'nice shirt on top' and 'pyjama pants on the bottom'.

What then is this story about? It was not, Lallie was careful to explain, about having a great case manager, although she regards herself as lucky in that regard, finding someone 'really willing to sort of listen and think of me as a whole person'. It is not a story about pluck, having a positive attitude, or hard work.

In Lallie's words, she insisted this was a story of relative 'privilege'. Lallie explains it thus: 'I have a background in advocacy. I just advocated for myself.' Lallie is a single mother, a refugee, an African Australian. We talked of her experiences of racism and sexism: 'I don't always sit in the privilege basket.' I was surprised by her choice of words, but also grasped that Lallie was intent on impressing upon me that she is more than the identity categories I might be tempted to tell her story through.

Lallie sees herself and takes pride in possessing 'system literacy privilege'. By this she means that through her work and over time she has accrued deep and valuable knowledge about how to navigate systems of support. Every time she made a call to Centrelink or a provider, for example, she made notes about who she spoke to and what she was said. She undertook research before meetings and arrived knowing her entitlements, just as foster mum Jo had done. Adept at navigating welfare bureaucracies, then, Lallie was able to wring resources out of a scenario that only harmed many other of my interviewees.

••

One of my interviewees distanced herself from those ParentsNext should ideally target and benefit: 'mothers abusing the welfare system'. And in Ceduna, I was offered insistent stories about those who really needed the card, which had been unfairly issued to *them*. Disassociation from highly stigmatised, mythical others emerges as a common feature of conditional welfare systems. In this way, suggests Richard Sennett, dignity is reclaimed, as people put distance between themselves and their social problems, pursuing life 'as more than a creature of circumstances'.²⁵

Indeed, in the United Kingdom, social researchers identify a long history of 'the poor' separating themselves from other more stigmatised categories of people in poverty. The Elizabethan Poor Law of 1601 famously instantiated a moral distinction between the deserving and undeserving poor. That is not to say these categories have been static since, but they have proved enduring. The imperative to distance oneself from less deserving poor people fluctuates over time, as does the particular form and content of the dissociation. In austerity times, where welfare spending has been cut in the midst of an aggressive discourse about 'benefit scroungers' and welfare fraud, poor Britons churn between low-wage jobs and unemployment and go without basic necessities such as heating. Yet they are reluctant to describe themselves as 'poor', stressing instead their 'pride in coping with hardship', a theme especially prominent in interviews with mothers. These impoverished Britons craft 'distancing narratives' from those they see as unwilling to work, fraudulent claimants to social security or profligate consumers who make bad decisions.[26]

Also writing about the United Kingdom, Ruth Patrick identifies that one of the ways some deflect the stigma of welfare receipt and establish their desert is pointing to migrants as undeserving.[27] This theme arose in one of my interviews. An interviewee complained that Australia seemed 'more sympathetic towards people who come in as refugees than we are to people of our own'. The government 'doesn't think twice' about helping someone 'from a war-torn country', but their claim on assistance was weak when contrasted to her circumstances. My interviewee complained, 'But actually, they haven't paid tax ever. So why are we offering them help?' Then, 'there are people who are doing it especially tough, having lost their jobs and are forced into a redundancy or have any sort of abuse in their past and they go from, you know, high taxpayers to now needing assistance. Um, there's a lot of prejudice around it.' She valorised taxpaying and cited her own formerly high contributions to establish the legitimacy of turning to the state for help because of circumstances beyond her control.

The comments about refugees' entitlement to social security are unfounded. Income support payments are in most cases available only to

Australian citizens and permanent residents. As an Australian government website explains: 'most migrants do not have access to the majority of payments for up to four years after their arrival'.[28] What I am pointing to is an observed effort on the part of 'welfare recipients' to distance themselves from other, less deserving categories of welfare recipients.

Australia is not austerity UK. Certain features are shared, and others diverge. While it is hard to be certain amid a highly fragmented media landscape, single mothers on welfare in Australia don't seem to attract intense and constant opprobrium—the 'pervasive negative visibility' Angela McRobbie identifies.[29] Instead, public censure seems more readily channelled towards those facing long-term unemployment. A powerful and negative discourse about unemployed people routinely surfaces in discussions about low-wage, piecemeal agricultural labour, for example. The agricultural supply chain in Australia is dependent on cheap labour imported temporarily from the Pacific, prompting representations of unemployed persons in Australia as work-shy.[30] Always mythological, this image of work-shy 'bludgers' is ever more disconnected from reality. In 2007, a JobSeeker recipient was typically a 'young, able-bodied man looking for work'. Today, they are likely to be older, to be a woman and to suffer from a chronic illness or disabilities that prevent them from working full-time but do not qualify them for the Disability Support Pension.[31]

∴

So far, I have elaborated themes my interviewees explicitly set before me. In closing, I turn to a more subterranean topic: the experience of becoming passive in the process of rendering an account of one's life. Historian Mark Peel eloquently describes the 'indignity of the investigation' into one's impoverished circumstances. For some of his interviewees, this was even more painful than the material penury they found ways to endure; they 'resented having to passively accept someone else's interpretation of their problems'.[32]

This is what Arlie told me: she was initially hopeful that ParentsNext might support her to attain her driver's licence, which her first case manager affirmed. The idea was dismissed by her next case manager, whom she met a month later. At a third appointment, with another case manager again, 'the lady asked me to tell her about myself'.

Arlie talked. Meanwhile, 'she was writing it all down [on] a blank piece of paper'. Arlie is a 'young mum'; she is 21 and has two kids. Her partner is an apprentice plumber. 'I'm proud of everything I have, although not everyone sees it that way, and I felt quite judged as she wrote down my life story.' Arlie continued, 'I don't know why but I cried about it that night.'

The blank piece of paper being imprinted by another's pen seemed to me a suggestive image. Arlie's story was rewritten in that moment to fit a policy narrative about 'teen pregnancy', 'educational attainment' and 'welfare dependence'. That's not the story that Arlie was telling, nor the story she lives by.

I heard echoes of this rewriting in Shelby's painful retelling of eligibility questions aimed at capturing a phenomenon that gets called 'intergenerational welfare dependency'. This was the one moment that she remembers most clearly from the initial phone call that established her eligibility: 'They said something about whether your parents had ever been out of work during your teenage years or something.' Shelby answered, 'Yes.' But there was a context to her answer, which was not captured by the eligibility survey.

Shelby explained to me, 'Because my dad's a builder and often he's out of work. But he doesn't go on the dole, as such, but yeah, the building industry's up and down all the time. So, you know, yes, he has been out of work.' The more complicated story then is this: Shelby's dad lost work in the 1990s recession, resorting to 'doing bits and pieces' for a time. These particular circumstances and his capacity to survive them were enveloped into a new, simplified narrative: Shelby became a 'welfare-dependent' single mother whose father was 'unemployed'. Shelby's own story, as it was narrated to me, is that she is an educated domestic abuse survivor slowly rebuilding a life in a coastal town with her son.

Ayesha, who grew up in Kolkata and holds two postgraduate degrees, enjoys a greater degree of social standing than Arlie or Shelby: she is highly qualified, speaks of a 'career' rather than 'work', which has a more instrumental cast, and has led a transnational cosmopolitan life that shaped the tenor of our rich exchange. It struck me that she held tightly to her own self-imagining, despite attempts at its rewriting.

Ayesha saw herself as more than a welfare recipient and more than a mother, 'as much as I love listening to *Peppa Pig* and *Paw Patrol* on repeat'. She liked to conjure an image of herself, she told me, 'that active, corporate-gear-wearing, you know, Starbucks-holding person who was taking the commute into the city every morning'. She referred to 'that bit of me' and also said, 'I've lost quite a bit of me.' Ayesha seemed poised to retrieve and foreground the parts of herself she valued. Others I interviewed had their story more strongly subsumed into the process of rewriting.

Yet Eloise too, who left school in Year 9 and lived with the 'dumb girls have babies' story, worked to subtly overwrite the tale of 'intergenerational welfare dependence'. As earlier explained, she was raised by a single mother. It was 'just me and my mum. Yeah. Just the two of us. Um, my dad kind of came and went occasionally, but it was, it was just the two of us'. She stated, 'So I am the next on the line of single parenting.' It was then that Eloise recast single motherhood from a source of lack to a source of strength. 'I respect my mum a lot for raising me as well as she could,' said Eloise. She did her very best 'with the resources … that she had'.

6

'They think we're rubbish'

Robby is among many who told me that they found the cashless debit card a 'bloody insult', felt 'targeted', and that they regarded their conscription into the card's first trial as 'degrading'. Beyond these common themes lie more specific life stories.

Robby's acute shame about being issued and using the card was bound up with recent historical dynamics and personal experiences. For Robby, the shame associated with carrying and presenting the card essentially restages early experiences of dealing with proximate white others' derisive gazes, their judgements and their taunting.

He began, 'I just feel like I'm another person to blokes that's got a regular job and me, pulling the card out in front of them, that's embarrassing. "Oh, he's on the card" … you know.' His story continued: 'So anyway … Yeah, you get your little smirks and stuff like that around the place, you know. Fellas thinking, "What are you on the card for?" Ask the government that! … They've given us the card because they've taken away our rights, simple as that.'

Drawn to the language of rights, Robby emphasised his equality with other 'blokes', communicating his familiarity with a masculine Australian vernacular. Another elderly Aboriginal person objected to the card on similar grounds. Stan insisted that the card represented an outdated way of treating Aboriginal people, a measure that properly belonged to an era before equal rights. 'We're gettin' educated now!' was his refrain, referencing a historical shift in the status of Aboriginal people from the 1960s onwards, which informed his objection to the card.

Robby was unemployed when I first spoke to him but soon after found work. And he was by no means idle when 'unemployed' and on the card: I caught up with him once as he vigorously swept out a yard with a stiff broom, as part of the 'mutual obligations' required of unemployed persons. On that occasion, he taught me the word for 'crow' in his language, Kokatha Gugada: ganga. That is, he was multiply busy, sweeping and being himself, sharing knowledge and insights into his whole world with me.

Across numerous other conversations, Robby reflected on a varied working life in manual jobs with intermittent periods of un- or under-employment. Working in mines produced ambivalence. The jobs were lonely and uncomfortable: 'I didn't really like it. It was, like, enclosed. I was in a smelter.' This work also produced discord: 'Nah, mining wasn't me. I'd rather be out in the paddock or out in the bush. You know. Look after country. Preserve it. Make sure that everything's OK for, like I mentioned the other day, the unborn.'

I relate Robby's experiences of waged work here to emphasise his self-understanding as just 'another person to blokes that's got a regular job' and to redress his painful experience of misrecognition when he pulled out the card. But what most struck me after talking with Robby was that he seemed especially attuned to the 'smirks and stuff' of others, perhaps because this scrutiny and contempt resonated with childhood experiences.

Robby relayed a story about schooling, which involved a shocking transition from community life on the Koonibba Lutheran Mission to a large high school. An older generation of Aboriginal people in Ceduna, to which Robby belongs, vividly recall the mission's end in 1963, which precipitated increased movement of Aboriginal people into regional towns and saw them come into more extensive contact with sometimes hostile townspeople.

At a national level, things were fast changing in this period. The 1967 referendum is popularly remembered as a vote on Aboriginal citizenship rights, as it provided for Aboriginal and Torres Strait Islander people to be counted in the national census, and granted the Commonwealth the power to legislate for First Nations people. While the overwhelming national 'yes' vote of more than 90 per cent today represents a powerful affirmation of the public's support for change with regard to Aboriginal and Torres Strait Islander issues, in Ceduna 48.45 per cent of voters cast a 'no' vote, out of a total population of 809.[1] This startling fact points to the reality of racial tensions in the region at this time. Robby's family faced these when they left the mission just before its end.

Like Uncle Bert, Robby grew up around Aboriginal men who worked on the railways and on nearby farms. However, Robby's dad was struggling to find work in the district, and they moved some distance away from the mission after he secured employment in the steelworks of a larger regional town. This transition involved going 'from being around, amongst, blackfellas, all my life' to becoming a minority and object of scrutiny and derision. 'I was just like … one little blackfella against, amongst, a [large] high school … you know? I'm the only one there. I just felt so alone.'

The taunting at school was compounded by his neighbours turning away from his family at home. 'I lived next door to an Aussie family and on the right side of me, the next door, I lived next to English, people from England, and I was sort of copping it left, right and centre: "black this" here, "black that" there.'

'Black this' and 'black that' were the terms Robby offered me. Clearly, 'this' and 'that' stood in for insults made in stronger language. Today, Robby casts those racist neighbours as the problem: 'I don't know whether they got educated while they were growing up, after I left school and after I left them, but … I'm hoping they did.' This empathetic and philosophical perspective was obviously not available to him as a teen. At 14, Robbie left high school because 'I pretty much had enough of all the racism'.

Stacey's shame was also pervasive but absent the racial dimensions of Robby's. Introduced earlier, Stacey is an aged-care worker. When I interviewed her, she was also studying online and raising young children alone. The moment she used the card to make a purchase, she felt immediately inveigled as—and reduced to—someone 'on Centrelink'. The kind of person about whom others, she worried, might be thinking 'should you really be out at the bakery having lunch?'

Some settings 'especially' produced this fear of scrutiny and judgement. Like the op shop. 'I really feel it there,' Stacey told me.

I said, 'I wonder why you feel it there?'

She replied, 'I don't know … because they're elder people and they're very well respected in the community … It makes me feel like I'm a drug user or something like that, because I'm on the card. Where it's not the case at all! So that's why I think that it's sort of stereotyped there that if you're on the card you're …' Stacey left the silence for me to fill in.

I met up with Brian on a beach. Also a whitefella, Brian sees himself as somewhat of an outsider who 'doesn't like drinking coffee with rednecks'. Sooty oyster catchers picked their way across bundled beds of seaweed, grey curled strips resembling cured bark. Brian told me passionately, 'I've never been a bludger, but I've been tarred.' Starting physical work alongside his dad as a teenager had worn out his body early. He was defensive about not working in his mid-fifties but also reasoned, 'I've done my time.' It was Brian who summed up the thought Stacey left unspoken: 'They think we're rubbish.'

••

Shame is a theme of many works dealing with life on welfare today across the Global North. Drawing on psychoanalytic thought, Richard Sennett explores the 'nakedness of shame'. Shame involves exposure; it often 'refers to losing control over what is being revealed'.[2] Above are depicted two such scenes of exposure: shame was generated in the moment that Robby handed over his card in the supermarket and when Stacey pulled hers out to pay for lunch in the bakery. In those moments Robby and Stacey became acutely aware of others' eyes resting on them, others becoming privy to information about them. Shame was also sometimes induced by me asking about it: the suggestion of shame becoming a source of it. A deeply embodied experience, shame can thus be hard to capture and grapple with by initiating conversations about it.

Yet shame is also more multifaceted than the awful feelings associated with exposure. I have written in depth on the topic of shame and welfare with sociologist Emma Mitchell.³ We urge an understanding of shame as shaped by history, as per Robby's story, as well as culture. We also see shame as always in flux. Shame is not a fixed, static thing—either present or absent. 'As much as it may haunt and stultify,' anthropologist Jennifer Biddle argues, 'shame also shapes and defines and makes for the very delineations called self-identity.'⁴ Shame thus violates boundaries between the public and private but also sharpens the boundary between oneself and another. Moreover, sources of shame are conditioned by the assumptions and commitments we hold, which shift across cultures, themselves mutable. This point will become clearer when I later consider the marked muting of the shame associated with the card to which many Aboriginal people in Ceduna directed my attention.

Sennett's writing on shame arises within his analysis of welfare bureaucracies. For Sennett, the route to both self-respect and mutual respect in American society is waged work. The same can be said of Australia. Certainly, the theme of the dignity of work was frequently present in my interviews. For example, when I interviewed Stephanie about her experience of ParentsNext, she reflected on the fact that she was the same age as her dad, an English migrant—a 'Ten Pound Pom'—who lost his job in the 1990s recession, more than a decade before he envisaged retiring. Struggling with the introduction of computers in his workplace, he never worked again. He was a 'gentleman' who wished to provide for his family. Stephanie's dad could not countenance welfare receipt and unravelled. As Sennett posits, 'welfare dependency' represents 'a synonym for humiliation'.⁵ Unemployment became the defining tragedy of Stephanie's dad's life. She soberly pondered what lay ahead for her at a very different but also strangely parallel juncture. She had stepped out of a demanding public service contract role that became unsustainable as she parented two young children alone, faced a crazy commute and looked after her elderly mother.

For Sennett, coming into contact with welfare bureaucracies as part of the search for assistance compounds the inherently demeaning situation of being out of work. Bureaucratic processes involve being subjected to a constant denial of respect 'as a full human being whose presence matters'.⁶

Sennett rightly points out that twentieth-century welfare bureaucracies replaced the invasive, discretionary and personalised systems of charitable relief that pre-dated them. He also captures how the experience of dealing with a rule-bound system and being treated at a distance—impersonally or overly bureaucratically—can also be deeply insulting. Dustin, for instance, reflected on the everyday, low-level humiliation that his Work for the Dole experience entailed. 'I sort of had a word with my last case worker,' he told me. 'I'm not signing a time sheet … because that's kind of insulting. I'm not signing that work sheet. They can visually see me here and these workers can give a verbal agreement that I attended my work hours, but it's wrong. I'm not signing that.' Dustin essentially refused to play along with the faux-job that the piece of paper that was his 'time sheet' came to represent. His refusal to participate in what he saw as a belittling and bureaucratic practice is echoed in others' efforts to repel or redirect shame. In this chapter, then, are featured scenes of exposure, humiliation and insult—or 'scorn', as Megan puts it below—be they associated with experiences of the welfare system or more broadly connected to receiving welfare.

••

Megan left her partner, thinking it in her daughter Phoebe's 'best interests'. Phoebe now sees her dad one day a week, which is better than subjecting her to 'seven days of toxicity'. Megan reflects that she had no idea she was stepping into a stigmatised role in society in becoming a single mother, full stop. Becoming a 'single mother on welfare' was another thing again.

'I never wanted to be a single parent. And here I am literally holding the baby 24/7, seven days a week and no family support. This was not the plan.' Megan never envisaged her partner, a highly driven financial adviser, would give up full-time work, but she did imagine returning to work part-time. That possibility receded.

'It never occurred to me to think that single mothers would be somehow seen as lesser than. Like it just didn't ever occur to me … it wasn't a concept, let alone a reality …'

There are a 'few sides to it,' Megan perceived. One dimension involves the fallout from an antagonistic break-up. Megan found herself living in a new part of Sydney and 'shunned from the one community I've known for eight or nine years. There was no space left for me—unfairly, no doubt about it. But that was the reality of it.' The resulting isolation was 'intensely painful'. Megan stated, 'I know I'm doing what's best for my child, but I'm not just struggling financially, I'm struggling socially.'

'I definitely felt the scorn and ejection, a lot.' She elaborated on what she lost. 'It's never said, it's never said.' That is, it's not explicit, but ... 'When suddenly you're sexually available—let's call a spade a spade—there's a threat level and the invitations dry off and you're no longer ...' No longer invited is what she meant. To put it differently, the people Megan knows do 'couples stuff': camping trips, dinners. Megan talked of 'grieving' the loss of her relationship, her idea of a family and also access to 'the social world of couples'.

Instead, Megan was drawn to and joined the world of other single mums, 'by necessity'. 'It's not the same as having family support' but proved akin to it. In fact, the support provided by a 'few key single mums' was critical. 'Without that I would have gone stir crazy, a long time ago. Absolutely.' Megan said, 'My single mum friends are my heroes in more than one way.'

Despite differences, Megan sensed a bedrock of commonality. 'You're working harder than you've ever worked in your life and still being somewhat socially scorned.' Megan loves her single mum friends and needs them; nevertheless she also related: 'It's such a small world and, all of a sudden, the only world I have. My professional sphere has gone. My social sphere, by and large, is gone. And I'm existing in this little hub called "single mums".'

Then there are the 'political' dimensions. 'So, you know, Centrelink, policies, blah, blah, blah. This is the whole ParentsNext thing.' Within the welfare system, Megan felt 'beyond judged'. A single mum receiving income support is 'definitely stigmatised and shamed'. She calls it 'a smear campaign to, to somehow, yeah, make women, mothers, feel less than'. For Megan, underlying social expectations are at work. 'Because the patriarchy says you should have kids with, you know, the one man who is their father, till death do us part, you know, obey thy husband: all that old stuff … If I just stayed in that relationship, would have been fine. None of us would've been on Centrelink, both of us would've been working. The social status would have been there. Everyone would've been happy.'

Megan added, 'My child would have been absolutely mentally and emotionally a basket case, in the long run. No doubt about it. Even [Phoebe's dad] acknowledges that. Like, that's how obvious it was …'

∴

Craig received a letter. He found it 'very blasé'. He was trying to get off the cashless debit card shortly after the first trial commenced in Ceduna in March 2016. This letter was from a Department of Human Services 'official', to use Max Weber's term, whose loyalty is to an office 'devoted to impersonal and functional purposes'.[7] Craig essentially received an impersonal letter—a bureaucratic response—explaining the rules. As Craig understood it, the letter said, 'Suck it up, piss off.' He had memorised this letterwriter's name; it rolled off his tongue when I first interviewed him in 2017. He kindly, if cheekily, suggested that they need something 'remedial': a lesson in 'how to deal with people in a better manner'.

While Craig tried unsuccessfully to exit the card trial via a personal request early on in the first trial, three more bureaucratic routes were later instituted to provide for the release he was seeking. The first of these was known as a 'wellbeing exemption'. This applied to Aero, who told me his prison stories. Recall that if being on card was deemed to pose a serious risk to a person's mental, physical or emotional wellbeing, they could be exempted from the program. As of June 2022, forty-eight people in Ceduna had applied for a wellbeing exemption, and thirty-five of these applications were approved. A mere 18 per cent of the approved applications were from Indigenous applicants.[8]

A second and distinct exemption process was instituted in 2019. Instead of revolving around the card's impact on an applicant's wellbeing, this process involved the applicant demonstrating personal 'responsibility'

A cardholder could apply to exit the program and come off the card on the grounds that they were financially responsible. In late 2019, I met up with a Filipina woman, Anne, while she was awaiting the decision on her exit application. She worked in a local casual job as well as caring for her husband. After submitting her application form, Anne received a follow-up phone call. The caller first read her application back to her, 'from a screen'. Then, as if trying to ferret out the truth, the caller demanded, 'What do you need cash for?'

Anne replied, 'Hang on. I don't mean to be rude, but why do you need to know that?' She explained to me that she wished to free up her funds in order to regain control of how she organises her money, which includes transfers to adult children, who remain in the Philippines. I am not sure whether her exit application was successful. As of June 2022, 312 people in Ceduna had applied via this second process to exit the long-running use of the card there. Only thirty-eight of these applications were approved and only 29 per cent of the approved applications were from Indigenous applicants.[9]

The third process I refer to provided for a variation to the terms of the card, rather than complete exemption. In Ceduna and the East Kimberley, the card's introduction involved the establishment of 'Community Panels' comprising local identities, who were tasked with assessing requests to vary the split of sequestered moneys on the card; that is, the card automatically quarantined 80 per cent of income support payments, and the remaining 20 per cent was paid into the recipient's bank account. The panel was empowered to grant up to 50 per cent of the applicant's social security payments to land in the recipient's bank account. It was this Community Panel process that I discussed most extensively with people.

A question-and-answer factsheet explained the Community Panel process thus: 'The panel members make a decision using the information on your application form and their own knowledge of the community.'[10] That is, these panel members might well be known to the applicant. Far from impersonal, this bureaucratic process involved disclosing intimate details to fellow community members. This was potentially a deeply exposing process, as emerges below.

First, applicants to the Community Panel had to answer a series of questions on a form. 'Paperwork is boring,' mused David Graeber. Yet, 'in most existing societies at this point, it is precisely paperwork, rather than any other forms of ritual, that is socially efficacious'.[11] Filling out this paperwork was potentially socially efficacious if severely constrained. For Tess Lea, a brilliant anthropologist of bureaucracy, the policy design cycle produces a 'surfeit of documents that are designed not to be read', so dense that 'they actively repel close attention'. The 'eye-glazing, unfriendly documentary hulk' of tenancy agreements, for example, results in paperwork that is not read by the people putatively addressed by the document as its readers.[12] By contrast, the Community Panel application form, as well as the paperwork about this paperwork, was plain-speaking and readable.

'Have you been convicted of an offence where alcohol, drugs or domestic violence were a factor in the past 12 months? Last term, did your child/ren miss more than one day a week of school on average? Have there been any substantiated child protection issues against you in the last 12 months?'[13]

'Have you applied to the Community Panel?' I asked Uncle Bert.

'No.'

'Do you know about it?'

'No.'

'Have you applied to the panel?' I asked Elisabeth.

'Um, I don't know how to go about that at the moment.'

I talked with white woman Rose, who began the application process but did not complete it. 'I don't need that kind of scrutiny.' As Dustin explained, 'There's a lot of people that won't go because there's personal problems. They do not have to tell a panel why they are stressed out! That is not the panel's or the government's business!' The risk of exposure for Rose, Dustin and others was too great.

Helen, whom I visited at home and who talked of the 'trepidation' she experienced while out shopping with the card, was determined to avail herself of an opportunity to present evidence about her circumstances. She told me this story. 'I was on eighty–twenty. Eighty per cent on the card and twenty per cent in my bank account.' Then someone said to her, 'You should go for the fifty–fifty.' She drafted an application.

Helen took her draft to the local employment services provider: 'Behind the bakery in the mall, yeah, in there. It's not their fault. The girls there are wonderful. Any time I've been in there, they've been just great and they've got the [cashless debit card helpline] number … they just dial it. They don't even have to look it up any more, so that's how often they have to ring it.'

'I had to take it in there and they looked it through and they said, "Oh, you won't have any problems at all. Look at this." Rah-rah-rah.' Then? 'Then I waited three months before I got a letter, in a second-hand envelope, that had stuff stuck over the previous … what it had been used for. It said, "You won't be getting your fifty–fifty, but we'll give you sixty–forty."'

Those 'girls', they were immediately available, affirming, familiar. But the panel's deliberations moved slowly, and the envelope was second-hand. A good recycling initiative perhaps, but it compounded Helen's sense of injurious and disrespectful treatment.

After interviewing Helen, I lodged a Freedom of Information request regarding Community Panel decisions in Ceduna. I learned that the Ceduna Community Panel had approved 140 applications as of 31 August 2018: at this stage, eight applicants had had their restricted amount reduced to 50 per cent; 80 applicants had had their restricted amount reduced to 60 per cent; and 52 applicants had their restricted amount reduced to 70 per cent.

While the Frequently Asked Questions were available in triplicate—a PDF version, a Word version, a soothing e-Voice version—the workings of the Community Panel remained opaque throughout its operations. 'You won't be getting your fifty–fifty, but we'll give you sixty–forty,' read Helen's letter in essence. No justification was given as to why she could be entrusted with 40 per cent of her Disability Support Pension in her bank account but not 50 per cent. She summed up: 'And to me, that's just a power trip.'

∵

When the administration of welfare and its conditions goes digital and bureaucratic treatment takes place outside personal interactions, shame seems less pronounced. However, as it recedes, anxiety assumes a heightened role. Shelby told me, 'The reporting I cannot stand. I have three different alarms in my phone to remind me to report and sometimes you get interrupted and then you just ... you totally forget and then you're not paid. Your rent's due, all my credit card repayments are due, my loan's due.' The anxiety associated with complying with digitised bureaucratic reporting requirements was a constant theme of my interviews with ParentsNext participants.

Megan tired of the 'constant reporting, which also takes a psychological toll, the constant reminder, constant stress, like the anxiety ... It's that constant threat of getting your money taken.' So motivated was she to escape the reporting regime that she negotiated to sign a new participation plan by enrolling in an online course, which required far less frequent reporting to confirm that she remained enrolled. Megan picked ... aromatherapy! I would not mock her interests except that Megan told me this with a kind of exasperated mirth.

Megan sketched in full for me the absurdity of her situation. She was undertaking casual contract teaching at a regional TAFE campus. We talked at some length about her students and their motivations to study. Yet she was told that the hours she spends working were not sufficient to exempt her from ParentsNext. As an educator, this offended me. But the actual hours you spend teaching in the classroom are based on many more spent preparing, I ventured. 'I knowwwwww!' she responded.

Next, Megan's ParentsNext case manager identified a 'long-term goal' for her: keep the teaching job. 'No shit, Sherlock.' Originally, Megan agreed to report that she was attending playgroup on a fortnightly basis, but as soon as compulsion entered her weekly routine with Phoebe, who has special needs, it 'drained the joy' out of playgroup. So, instead, when I met her she was dipping in and out of a 'random aromatherapy course' and had been released from the demands of fortnightly reporting.

Here's Ayesha: 'I had to set up reminders on my phone ... to log into the Centrelink app to make sure I've ... confirmed that I've worked for zero hours, I have earned zero dollars. Um, so that was just a reminder that I'd put on my phone ... I don't remember to log in, if I've skipped a week, then any payments stop. Straight away.'

Shelby added, 'And like, I don't even have WiFi. I sort of had it on minimum, like not really much data, as well, my phone, just to kick my costs down, but I've had to increase that and have internet just in case. All that sort of stuff.'

It was Ayesha who pinpointed something other interviewees circled around: 'It sometimes felt like a game of, you know, they are trying to catch me doing something wrong.' Trish was even more blunt: 'I feel like I have a target on my back.'

••

Eloise also had a lot to say about the stigmatisation of single motherhood, but she felt the sting differently from Megan. She reasoned, 'Two people are not enough to raise a child. One person going to work and one person raising a child is not enough. Um, it's a cliché, but it does take a village. It takes a village to support a mum ... and it takes a village to raise a child.' Eloise has assembled that 'village': 'I'm lucky enough to have a whole bunch of friends who love my kid as much as I do. Um, and he's lucky enough to have four sets of grandparents, because we've—everyone's split up before then. So we've got quite a few involved.'

She continued, 'I'm lucky to have friends who I can go to their house and say, "I hate him today." And they go, "Yeah, that's all right." And that's fine ... And I think if you don't have that, you're wrecked.'

If it's hard enough raising children as a couple, then 'one person is not enough and it doesn't matter how good you are a parent, if you don't have a support network, you can't be a good parent. And I don't say this to malign single parents, I think it's just a fact.' This observation is derived from Eloise's experience of her break-up, which ushered in a period of isolation and grief. 'And I could not be a good parent.'

In that period, Eloise faced what she saw as a specific form of social stigma, 'housing stigma'. She remembered, 'No one wants to put a single parent and a young child in a rental. They just don't because kids wreck houses and that's their investment and they don't want you in there, especially when there's—you know, a working couple, [who] want the house. Why would they put the welfare mum in there?'

But more broadly, Eloise rejected the idea that she carried a social stigma. 'I haven't felt it and I think part of that is I was already a dropkick ... I was the smart kid that dropped out of school. I don't have my HSC. I had a baby young.'

Being a young single mum, however, came with pressures to transcend the shameful associations with that category. 'I think especially as a single mum, there is a pressure for me to go to uni or to get a job or to be doing something like that. And I want—I want to be house mum. I want to stay at home.' Eloise told me simply that she 'likes' it. Yet there's 'no room socially to do that'. What she is saying is that single mums who receive social security income are not entitled to decide that they want to commit themselves to periods of stay-at-home parenting in the early years, whereas this decision is socially sanctioned for middle-class parents.

Eloise elaborated on her decision to be a stay-at-home mum: 'I'm doing a job that if I was doing it for someone else's child [working in a childcare centre], I would be getting paid $30 an hour and I'm doing it 24/7 coz I chose to and I'm OK with that.' If she were 'receptive' to stigma, she thinks she would feel more strongly how unacceptable it is for a young single mother to elect to dedicate herself to parenting in the pre-school years, choosing unpaid work over low-paid work.

Eloise sensed the shame this decision invites but sloughed it.

••

Maude frowned and thought hard about whether the cashless debit card was a source of shame. 'Just usual, I suppose,' she began. 'Like the Medicare card and everybody uses that. Like that to me, you know, you're not shame,' she supplied.

This shrugging off of the shame surrounding the card was echoed by many of the Aboriginal people I spent time with, especially Pitjantjatjara-speakers, whose ancestral country lies in Ceduna's desert hinterland. Engaging these research participants on the topic of kunta (shame) did not produce lengthy or emotionally charged responses: 'not really' came one typical answer before the conversation was redirected to aspects of the card that did concern them.

One way of delving into the reason for this response is to consider Indigenous-specific sources of shame in the pre-Invasion past. Earlier generations of anthropologists describe Aboriginal people as living in small-scale, mobile societies whose members subsisted on hunted, gathered and collected food sources. These were essentially egalitarian societies, in which the cooperative effort demanded to sustain them placed a high value on both group cohesion and autonomy or individuality, as distinct from individualism.[14]

For the linguist Jay Arthur, shame is a central concept in Aboriginal English, but 'a difficult term to translate into non-Aboriginal English'. Arthur summarises three culturally inflected meanings of the term 'shame' as it is used today: 'embarrassment; fear; a sense of having transgressed the social and moral code of society, intentionally or unintentionally'.[15] Public attention, notes Arthur, might cause 'shame' as it transgresses an emphasis on 'social cohesion' and equality rooted in those pre-contact values.[16]

In keeping with Arthur's contemporary usage, shame might refer to an experience of being distinguished as an individual, for good or bad reasons. For example, I talked with a young person who collected a NAIDOC Week award on stage on behalf of a relative, in front of a gathered audience of community members. The experience of accepting the award was described to me as 'shame' and the attendant excruciation was expressed through a slight writhing. This was simultaneously a joy-filled and proud moment. To be on the card, then, when so many near others were on the card, was to belong. It did not transgress a shared moral code and thus did not produce shame.

It is also productive to turn to other examples where the shame usually associated with welfare receipt is relatively absent. Melanie Baak conducted research with Dinka refugee women resettled in Australia after she married into the community. Baak emphasises the intense obligation these women feel towards kin left behind in Africa. Baak does mention that many of her research participants are 'reliant on welfare payments', while others worked part-time, but makes clear that this dependence itself is not a source of shame.[17] Rather, it is the shame associated with their inability to acquit their responsibilities to family in need that haunts them.

Another instructive account comes from the United States. Karen McCormack explores what differentiated experiences of 'welfare stigma' among women receiving single-mother payments one year after the passage of Clinton's 1996 welfare reforms across two locations: one inner-city impoverished setting, one mixed-class rural/suburban county. She found that women living in mixed-class communities felt the stigma of welfare more keenly compared to women living in the inner city surrounded by other poor people. The women residing in the inner city 'described living in neighbourhoods where welfare receipt was taken for granted and seemed to expect that most other communities in the United States resembled their own'.[18] Living among other poor people also meant the inner-city women were more likely to 'understand poverty as a condition of their social group rather than a primarily individual affliction'.[19] She argues that inner-city women do not live in the 'same discursive space' as those who stigmatise them and so are less harmed by this stigmatisation.[20] So while the association between shame and welfare may be pervasive, its effect, reach and internalisation are uneven and depend on the social context and commitments of the communities in which stigmatised individuals dwell.

Finally, and moving closer to the scenario I am discussing, anthropologist Elizabeth Watt lived in the Cape York community of Hope Vale for a year in 2013. She learned that those people most likely to be placed on the BasicsCard there were Guugu Yimidhirr people deeply embedded in relations with kin. These 'embedded' people were also least likely to experience the BasicsCard as shame inducing or to object to the policy of income management, which disproportionately affected them. On the other hand, those community members who were more 'engaged' with the wider world beyond Hope Vale were more likely to express opposition to income management, even though they were less likely to be subject to it. While this might appear puzzling at first, Watt teases out divergent experiences of the contemporary world with deeper colonial roots, such that only some Guugu Yimidhirr people aspire to the kinds of respectable and 'responsible' ways of life the BasicsCard is meant to foster. Others are unconcerned by the inference that Aboriginal people lack these values, or the fact that they are individually deemed to lack them.[21]

The complexities associated with the relationship between being on welfare, using the card and shame are barely acknowledged within the advocacy-oriented scholarship dealing with the card's introduction in Ceduna and other remote Indigenous locales. This is understandable: a muting of shame in some cases is obviously hard to absorb into the kind of simplified narrative necessary for political debate. However, as Emma Mitchell and I have emphasised, the process of simplification comes with a casualty.

The perhaps surprising complexity of shame I document here provides an opportunity to recognise the specificity of the emphasis on the relationship between waged work and socially valued existence. To be clear, Pitjantjatjara-speakers have long been enmeshed in settler colonial economies and commodity exchange via dingo scalping, work on pastoral stations and recent decades of work within the organisational sector: they are not outside capitalism. However, no shame is attached to not being a wage-earner, even when conditional welfare measures serve to heighten the distinction between a waged worker with full citizenship rights and a welfare-dependent person whose everyday life is subject to a paternalistic intervention. Like the Dinka Australian women Baak describes, it is other attributes and commitments that hold more value. Cameo Dalley makes a similar observation about the East Kimberley cashless debit card trial site. Dalley perceives a 'labour of endurance' on the part of First Nations people, who remained determinedly oriented to relations among kin despite policy interventions designed to change them.[22]

7

'Had to be done'

In an American nail salon, the most common English word spoken is 'sorry'. The poet Ocean Vuong observed this refrain while watching his Vietnamese-born mother at work. 'Again and again', Vuong saw manicurists, 'bowed over a hand or foot' apologise, 'when they had done nothing wrong'. The word 'sorry', Vuong came to understand, 'insists' and 'reminds': 'I'm here, right here, beneath you.'

The invisibility of certain workers and the work they do, painfully and subtly evoked by Vuong's portrait of refugee women 'in the service of beauty', is a theme in other studies of feminised low-wage work.[1] When journalist Barbara Ehrenreich cycled through a series of poorly paid jobs in America two decades ago now, she noted a neediness for approval in some of her co-workers: a 'morsel of praise' might be savoured 'for weeks'. She concluded this stemmed from 'chronic deprivation'. Part of a team that cleaned houses while their middle-class owners were absent, Ehrenreich realised that these 'home owners aren't going to thank us for a job well done'. For research, she undertook work that was 'invisible and even disgusting': others undertook this work out of necessity.[2] When Australian journalist Elisabeth Wynhausen embarked on a similar exercise she realised this: office cleaning, which commenced before everyone left for the day, was physically demanding and also asked of her an effort to be 'inconspicuous'.[3]

Inconspicuous, invisible; physical. Necessary, constant. Pedicures, admittedly, are not vital to the maintenance, continuance and 'repair' of our world, to loop back to Fisher and Tronto's definition of care.[4] The cleaning of dishes, homes, offices and streets is. So too is the stacking of supermarket shelves and the tending of dependent bodies, of sick people and children. COVID-19 outbreaks drew attention to this critical daily work, which was officially designated 'essential', and to the people doing it in risky circumstances: working-class people; brown people; women, in the case of childcare and aged care.

The labour of looking after fragile and otherwise dependent others is a specific subset of this invisible work. Caring work 'had to be done', Gladys says below. It has to be done. Many of my interviewees narrated time spent undertaking work of this kind. Much of this was unpaid work, some of it was paid.

••

Gladys met her husband as a teenager. His ancestral country lay far away from hers; he was passing through the district. We talked of their romance.

Gladys's husband was 'bedridden for the last six months of his life'. At this point, Gladys found herself 'constantly on the go'. She ran me through the routine: 'As soon as he got up and had a shower, the bed was stripped, made, ready for him to jump back into cool, fresh sheets. I did this religiously every day.' Also, 'I made sure his meals were all cooked and ready.'

Gladys's description of these tasks and others, performed for a person she loved, captures taxing care work in circumstances that merged the physical work of caregiving with the emotional effort of caring about. 'I sort of never stopped and had time for myself,' she recalled. 'I got to clean the house and make sure the dishes were done. Washing had to be done. It was a continual six months of hard slog.'

Gladys was previously employed at the local family violence safe house, washing linen and just being 'there for women if they needed anything', like toilet paper or washing powder. 'They'd come to me, even if they just wanted to talk.' She had also worked as a cleaner in the past but stopped work to look after her terminally ill husband.

'When he passed away, it was just like hitting a brick wall. Everything come to a stop.'

Gladys found the local Centrelink employees, some of whom she was related to, 'compassionate'. Still, 'I really had a hard time going in there myself ... letting them know that my husband's passed away, that you have to stop this.' To ensure his social security payments ceased? I clarified. 'Yeah.' That meant Gladys, too, had her Carer Payment stopped.

Worn out and grieving, she was moved onto the unemployment payment and its attendant reporting requirements. 'Said I had to keep clocking in.' She was also issued the cashless debit card, which sequestered 80 per cent of her income in order to ensure its responsible use.

∴

Like Gladys, June too had shifted from paid care work to unpaid care work. A grandmother and foster carer, June proudly explained to me the vocational qualification she holds as an aged care worker, describing this work as 'really rewarding'. She talked to me of 'winning the hearts' of elderly white patients who 'didn't like Nungas'.

Then June became the carer for her elderly mother, whom she nursed until her death. June's attempts to re-enter the workforce since then were frustrating: 'Since I've turned 60 it's really hard to get a job.' She too found herself on the card.

Importantly, after a lifetime spent shouldering the responsibility of looking after people, in paid and unpaid capacities, June expressed her primary objection to the card as follows: 'They're taking the responsibility away from me. From my life, I reckon ... It's treating me like a little kid again.' June is adept at caring for others; the assumption that she is incapable of taking good care of herself rankled. For whatever reason, June identified and articulated this insult more pointedly than Gladys did. Her critique is echoed in other studies of compulsory income management, with many subject to it describing that 'they felt infantalised and demeaned appealing to the generosity of others in a way that they didn't when accessing state entitlements'.[5]

Gladys and June gravitated towards feminised, low-wage roles throughout their long working lives before ending up on the cashless debit card. The ParentsNext participants I interviewed, who were generally aged in their twenties and thirties, talked of undertaking similar work before and in between having children.

Anna, for example, who was newly mandated to partake in ParentsNext when I interviewed her, described her work in a spinal cord injury unit. 'When I left the bad relationship—my first long-term relationship—I had to start from scratch.' At the time she had 'two young sons'. She knew that 'I had to get into my own rental'. She also knew that 'I wouldn't be able to afford … well, not on my own'. Again, in an economy structured around two incomes and high housing costs, sole parenting exposes one to the risk of poverty. Anna continued, 'But I needed to be able to become financially independent … so that I could provide for my kids.' She enrolled in a home and community service course. 'That's where it all began.'

June and Anna helped me to understand that as much as waged care work is underpaid, undervalued and challenging, it can also be deeply meaningful work. Anna cares for people accessing social services rather than people she already cares about, as Gladys and June detailed. Still Anna told me, 'I love it.' She continued, 'I do love helping people.' Anna elaborated, 'It's nice to be able to help somebody at least somewhat be, you know, independent in a way, without having to rely on their family all the time. And you know, everybody's got their own goals in life, so helping people achieve that. And you know, obviously providing quality care.' It was 'hard work,' she reflected, which involved demanding physical labour. 'But I love my job, I do, and I really … I'm really grateful for the people that I work with.'

Ella, too, described working as a teacher's aide as simultaneously low status, 'unstable', a 'dead end' and 'lovely'. When I interviewed her, Ella had been working intensively with a traumatised child. On one occasion, this child 'had a huge episode … [W]e ended up on the floor in each other's arms crying on each other.' This proved a breakthrough moment, and a slow process of integration into the classroom began after it.

Ella secured this job through personal connections—a friend who is a teacher posted the opportunity on Facebook. She moved off an income support payment and was able to exit ParentsNext. Yet her ParentsNext provider 'took full credit' for her finding employment, 'and they got their bonus'.[6] In fact, after Ella informed them that she had secured work she received a letter from her provider. It stated that they had found her a job. This letter also instructed her to attend work.

∴

In Sydney's 2020 autumn lockdown, I visited my aunt to go walking with her and take her meals. In winter 2021, Sydney entered a longer and harsher lockdown, especially in the poorer and super-multicultural suburbs of Western and south-western Sydney where I happen to live. My local Member of Parliament, Tony Burke, later wrote about 'the unfair treatment of our area during the lockdown', pointing out that, 'We are the home of essential workers—those who couldn't just sit at home during the pandemic and work from a laptop.'[7] I was of course sitting at home over this period, writing this book on a laptop, acutely conscious of my privileged circumstances as helicopters hummed in the background. The critical and difficult care labour undertaken by aged-care workers was especially on my mind because my aunt had recently moved into an aged-care facility.

There were occasions in the preceding year when I stood by her side as she attempted to open her front door with a $50 note. 'Not this one!' she might say, before fishing around in her handbag for $20 or her public transport card to attempt to thread it through the keyhole. While dementia first affected her relationship with language, her relationship with objects was also clearly deteriorating. She pointed to some knobbly lemons dangling from her tree, admiring 'the onions'.

All of those who cared for her over this time, keeping her company and surreptitiously undertaking vital tasks, intuitively grasped that our job was to keep an illusion of independence and competence intact. 'The other one's a good one,' I might say casually, summoning patience on the doorstep and gesturing towards keys. My skills were evolving in response to my aunt's needs, which were as much existential as they were practical.

The view that working with old people or with children is 'unskilled', I came more fully to appreciate, is surely only expressed by those who have never been consumed by it.

The word 'help' enraged her. The mention of organised 'activities' demeaned her. Her imitations of anyone who spoke to her slowly and with sucrose fakery were catty and hilarious. Those professionals we managed to engage for the purpose of diagnosis—minor deception was involved in the orchestration of these encounters—were called 'ridiculous' and 'stupid' after they left. Indeed, she asserted her dignity through anger, accessing an observed lucidity lacking from other muddled conversations.

My aunt's reluctance to accept the help she so clearly needed was frustrating, and I sometimes found it hurtful. I reminded myself that it did not so much point to an individual peculiarity on her part—although she certainly prized independence as a highly successful single woman. It was instead a symptom of a larger cultural problem with facing our neediness and reliance on others. This theme is of central import to this book. I opened by reflecting on disavowed and abhorred dependencies and return to further explore the status of dependency in debates about welfare below.

We placed my aunt in a reputable facility, where the staff quickly demonstrated that they had no grasp of her specific condition and needs. Indeed, the pandemic has brought the issue of institutionalised aged care into full public view. Many have been confronted with the horrifying realisation that the task of caring for elderly people—our people—has been marketised, falls overwhelmingly to women and is chronically undervalued.[8]

As I walked deserted, depressing corridors, weaving my way between her room and the front desk to complete the admission process, frail residents with paper-thin skin clinging to their cheeks peered at me. 'Are you my family?' one asked inquisitively, with hope. I found the balled and labelled socks of the room's former resident, presumably deceased, still rolling around a bottom drawer. A 'shortage of knowledge or skill' impeded this facility's capacity to look after my aunt.[9]

My aunt is a stylish dame. Within 24 hours, she strode out the door in knee-high black leather boots and police were called. Long story short: a stressful month passed after this incident until we finally found an aged-care facility with the expertise and resources to look after my aunt respectfully.

∴

In the United States, the 1990s welfare reform agenda was advanced via a focus on a particular mythical figure, which had emerged in the previous decade: the Black 'welfare queen'. Hardly 'the most privileged of social subjects', Black single mothers were depicted as 'a nonproductive rentier class'.[10] That is, they were attacked as idle, even indolent and parasitically living on unearned moneys in the form of social security benefits. More broadly, the focus was on 'welfare dependence', which posited that reliance on social security corroded a recipient's character. Welfare was depicted as addictive, or as a 'poison', to return to Noel Pearson's lexicon.

Dependency, as noted in chapter 3, thus emerged as one of the welfare reform era's key words. Its negative connotations intensified throughout the transition from post-war capitalism to the new economic order, which saw the movement of women into the workforce en masse, as well as increasingly precarious workers and desiccated welfare systems. Numerous thinkers have carefully tracked the heightened role that the term 'dependency' has assumed in Australian debates about the causes of and solutions to disadvantage since the 1990s.[11] Taking an even longer view, scholars Nancy Fraser and Linda Gordon shed light on the shifting cultural associations with dependency over time.

In pre-industrial usage, they first establish, dependency was a normal condition of social relationships determined by status hierarchies. 'Neither English nor US dictionaries report any pejorative uses of the term before the early twentieth century,' Fraser and Gordon observe. Rigid status hierarchies meant that 'dependency' was the proper condition of the slave and serf.[12] Writing of the Elizabethan Poor Law of 1601, they note that it was certainly already 'shameful to ask for public help'. However, 'the culture neither disapproved of dependency nor valorized individual independence'. Poor laws aimed to ensure that the 'mobile, uprooted and excessively "independent" poor' return to their 'local parishes or communities and, hence, to enforce their traditional dependencies'.[13]

The associations with dependency shifted with the rise of industrial capitalism. Independence for male white waged workers was valorised, dependency becoming a 'deviant and stigmatized' condition. Also, dependency no longer always referred 'to a social relation; it could also designate an individual character trait'. In more concrete terms, 'certain dependencies became shameful while others were deemed natural and proper'.[14] Dependency was the desired condition of the wife, notably. Through the image of the 'housewife', dependency was feminised and further derided as unacceptable for men.[15] The associations with dependency were redrawn again as second-wave feminism contested wives' economic dependency and demanded middle-class women's entry into the labour force.

In contemporary Global North societies, all forms of dependency are now rendered 'avoidable and blameworthy', a general assumption fuelling that intensely contemptuous depiction of 'welfare dependency' in 1980s America, which also travelled to Australia.[16] Welfare dependency, Lawrence Mead and others argued, caused moral/psychological dependency. Dependence bred passivity: the passive must be 'activated', another of the welfare reform era's watchwords.

Scrutiny settled in America on impoverished Black single mothers, who had previously been denied assistance in parallel to Aboriginal people's limited access to the provisions of Australia's twentieth-century social security system. Richard Sennett sheds further light on the invocation of dependency as deeply shameful throughout welfare debates. For Sennett, this represents a 'horror of the primal maternal scene: the infant sucking at the mother's breast'. The fear is this: 'through force or desire, adult men will continue to suckle; the mother's breast becomes the state'.[17] It is in fact all adults to whom this statement applies.

A range of social reforms, in addition to welfare reform, also drew on the critique of dependency that gained ground in this era. Historian Barbara Taylor writes of her institutionalisation in a decaying Victorian-era London asylum in the late 1980s without romanticising its horrors: she found here a place where the 'threat of physical violence' was 'omnipresent'.[18] It was also a sanctuary—an asylum in the true sense of the word, which saved her life. Deinstitutionalisation was in full swing at this time. 'The guiding principle behind this vision was that the best way of life—for everyone, sick or well—was one of personal independence.'[19]

The asylum system was condemned for many legitimate reasons and at the insistence of courageous advocates who used mental health services and who fought to have their integrity, decision-making powers and dignity restored. Undeniably, however, the condemnation of these institutions was also energised by the argument that open-ended, long-term care fostered dependency. 'Today this independence imperative is stronger than ever,' writes Taylor. 'To need other people on a day-to-day basis (except in the case of the very young, very old or very disabled) is a mark of emotional debility,' she concludes.[20] The solution to institutionalisation in the United Kingdom and in Australia was 'community care'. In reality, as neoliberal priorities stripped funding from social infrastructure, family members were expected to assume care of those in need. And being cared for in the community 'has almost always meant care by women'.[21]

Contemplating the meaning and status of dependency today is not to long for a feudal system, feel nostalgic about rigid racial hierarchies or abusive asylums, or regret feminism's remaking of societies. Further, Fraser and Gordon's genealogy has American specificities. In terms of the Australian debate, the racialised single mother has not featured as strongly emblematic of welfare dependence.

A number of other stereotypes have instead circulated in Australian debates and media representations. Three come readily to mind. The young, supposedly unmotivated 'dole bludger' is one of them. Second, when I interviewed Anna about ParentsNext she told me about a friend of hers, a single mother with five children, and how 'judged' her friend felt. Anna contrasted her own relatively benign treatment with her friend's experiences. As a single mother on social security with more than three children, Anna's friend's sexuality was clearly treated as excessive and irresponsible.

The other potent image to circulate within welfare debates in Australia, and one that is especially relevant to this book, is that of a violent Aboriginal man. Analysis of the parliamentary debates surrounding income management tools such as the BasicsCard and the cashless debit card show a consistent representation of 'racialised male welfare recipients as objects of fear'. As touched upon in chapter 4, the card was frequently justified on the basis that it offered protection from the vociferous demands of kin. These debates also 'positioned white Australia as having a moral obligation to save these women and children'.[22]

A complex debate surrounds the cultural underpinnings of 'humbug': the compulsion to share individually held resources with kin empowered to assert a claim to them, in some Aboriginal settings.[23] Indeed, an Indigenous friend once explained to me that she had spent the day busily looking after an elderly companion who had just been paid and was worried others would 'rush at her', seeking access to her cash. Yes, this suggests an unwelcome pressure to redistribute her moneys. But another reality still is captured in that story, which is seldom made visible within welfare debates. My friend undertook unseen work here, committing a day to being with and caring for the interests of a vulnerable companion. Offering one's protective presence to another is an important job.

∴

What of those single mums I interviewed, many of whom had dependants to care for full-time? How did they experience the work of care and how did ParentsNext impede or support their caring efforts?

'A complete waste of my time,' concluded Lauris about ParentsNext. And recall that Kylie said to me, 'Many times I have arrived and my case worker went home early or didn't go to work that day without calling me or cancelling.' Natasha described waiting for an appointment with her toddler. 'There was nothing there. There was just a lounge for her to sit on and it was just lucky that … she'd taken a doll and I'd taken a little container with some Legos in it and yeah, to keep her occupied.' Natasha waited for an hour. Her daughter was 'bored and tired and wanting to go' long before the full hour elapsed.

These stories and others got me thinking about time. What does it mean to be absorbed, all the time, in parenting a dependent being? What is the relationship between this particular kind of care work and the conditional welfare system described in this book?

In general, 'contemporary unemployment' is a site of 'intense activity'.[24] However, conditional welfare rests on the assumption that when not undertaking mandated and surveilled tasks, welfare recipients' time is unoccupied: their days lie otherwise fallow, their hours ready to be filled with others' plans for their time, which always override their own allocation of time. Hence, my conversations with women about waiting for appointments to begin and to receive high-stakes phone calls. Two distinct but related things are happening here, which are worth teasing apart.

First, the amount of time it takes to parent is erased. Busy single mums talked to me about the ever-present and often conflicting claims on their time. Lefa described the 'struggle' associated with the 'five o'clock part of the afternoon'. She was constantly torn: 'Do I spend another 20 minutes jumping on the trampoline with [her son] or do I use that 20 minutes to add another three vegetables [to] the dinner?' As in, 'Do I stop playing ... now so that I can make these, you know, really nutritious meals that take an hour to cook ... and like what will he be doing in that time? Do I plonk him in front of a screen or do I try to get him to sit up at the island bench and get him to do some drawing?'

This, Lefa perceived, was the dilemma of the sole parent, who has to fulfil every dimension of the parenting role simultaneously. Megan described the exhaustion at the end of each day: 'When push comes to shove, at eight o'clock at night, when [Phoebe's] in bed, I just want [to be] a zombie. I just want to sit on the couch, eat chocolate and browse my phone.' One voice in her head told her to be more productive in this time; another responded that this was her only chance to 'zone out': 'Just to have that break.'

The caring tasks associated with 'keeping my baby alive', as Svetlana put it in our raw exchange, take time to acquit. Feeding, settling, cooking, cleaning, tidying, playing: these are essential tasks that fill hours. Further, a number of my interviewees described more time-consuming parenting routines still, because their children had particular needs associated with disability. Lallie joked to me that alongside her consultancy, she was also engaged in running her youngest child's 'corporation'. She was constantly driving him to appointments: 'It feels like I have a calendar just for him.'

It's not just that parenting is time-consuming, however. Parenting involves a specific orientation to or experience of time. In the early months of being a mother, novelist Rachel Cusk writes, her role was akin to a 'kidney': she processed waste. Motherhood, for Cusk as an artist, involved the loss of 'reams of unscripted time upon which I used to write my days, bearing the burden of their authorship'.[25] While the primacy of bodily processes that Cusk details fades as babies grow (and 'reams of unscripted time' describe very few people's working lives), parenting involves an experience of time still oriented to organic processes throughout the early years. That is, looking after small children involves being attuned to another's bodily rhythms: in Cusk's terms, these days are not 'sole-authored'.

This particular experience of time—being attuned to another's embodied and ever-evolving rhythms—is in tension with the organisation of time within conditional welfare. Today's welfare system runs on 'Appointment time', argues Karen Soldatić. She explains, 'The idea of the Appointment is clearly associated with ... clock time and calendar time.' This is the regulated time of capitalist work, which has been internalised. The capital-A Appointment is set for a 'specified time' set in the future, 'within a day, week, month and year'.[26]

In everyday life, appointments are set for agreed times mutually convenient to all parties involved. The appointments associated with conditional welfare regimes are decided unilaterally and their details provided to the welfare recipient alongside a threat. Recall, for example, Svetlana's story about the 'phantom phone call'. She was informed she would receive a phone call, which constituted an 'Appointment', and warned that if she failed to answer it, her payment would be suspended. When that call didn't arrive on time, her 'heart was missing a beat'. The phone call came instead hours later as Svetlana was in the process of picking up her daughter from pre-school. In other words: she was busy!

Yet Svetlana was inveigled as passive, still waiting, unengaged. Svetlana was well aware that ParentsNext is integrated with the Targeted Compliance Framework, which means that 'mutual obligation failures' result, automatically, in one's income being stopped. In fact, both a 'failure to attend (or be punctual for) an appointment the person is required to attend' constitutes a 'mutual obligation failure'.[27] That stipulation for punctuality in brackets is significant. It reflects the power relations inherent within waiting. One party can reasonably be expected to wait; the other cannot be kept waiting. Svetlana took the call, juggling the pick-up.

Soldatić's research participants, who were on the Disability Support Pension, talked of repetitive and worthless appointments, which they were required to attend, a phenomenon familiar to me. Importantly, Soldatić also shows that the 'pace of the impaired body' encompasses 'time-intensive practices of self-care' that are overridden by and are in tension with Appointment time's rigidity.[28] The pace of parenting is also tied to bodily processes, although not so much one's own. Infants need feeding and their nappies need changing, and the process of settling them for daytime sleeps at just the right time can come to punctuate whole days. It's this reality of being-attuned-to-another's-body time that is negated by Appointment time. Ayesha, for instance, ended her eligibility phone call appointment by simply acquiescing to the caller's misguided instructions. The reason? Her daughter 'was waiting for her next feed'.

Other interviewees talked of entering physical spaces that could not support the work of caregiving they were absorbed in: Arlie described to me her distress at having to change a nappy in a toilet cubicle at her provider's office. When Natasha and her toddler arrived for their appointment and were kept waiting, there was nothing there to play with.

A final example connects these reflections on the amount of time parenting takes and the experience of time it involves. A 49-year-old father of two children on the autism spectrum, who was then a compulsory ParentsNext participant, detailed his experiences for the 2019 Senate Inquiry. He described his three-year-old daughter 'having the run' of the reception area while his appointment proceeded. He was anxious about the various cords and cables within reach, as the open-plan space housed computers for client use. Further, 'I explained and was ignored when I detailed the time commitments I already have,' this father wrote. 'For example, in the 25 business days preceding the appointment … I had to attend 23 separate medical appointments with/for various family members.' With his daughter 'running around the offices', his participation plan was formulated and signed, in a 'state of stress'.[29]

Natasha's daughter played quietly with a doll and Lego rather than running around: she was 'tired' and in need of sleep. The dad who took the time to write a lengthy submission to the 2019 Senate Inquiry remained conscious of his daughter's energetic little body, needing to move. In both cases, parenting involved being attuned to another's bodily rhythms and needs, which Appointment time rudely cut across.

∴

We were all once vulnerable and will be again. We begin our lives in a condition of dependency as soft, squishy babies and are, we hope, nourished by our caregivers. We deteriorate and become more dependent again: hopefully this happens in old age. As Sennett identifies, the critique of dependency involves a repudiation of the primal scene. What might be learned by turning towards rather than away from the image of the baby suckling at the breast? What might flow from the acceptance of dependency?

British psychoanalyst Donald Winnicott regarded this critical period of early dependence and intensive caregiving as crucial in fostering autonomy. When the baby gazes into the mother's face, it should ideally see, according to Winnicott, not the face of another but the love and attention the mother has for that baby reflected in it.[30] To be clear, while Winnicott exclusively writes 'mother', it is the role and practices associated with mothering rather than the identity that emerges as important. It is my assumption that the 'mother' Winnicott describes can be a dad, a non-binary parent or a carer; 'the breast' Winnicott describes can be a bottle or a chest.

Winnicott also shows that slowly the baby learns to differentiate between itself and the mother figure, coming to see this figure as separate, as flawed but ideally reliable. If the mother is dependable or 'good enough', then the baby learns to play and be alone—the mother's reliability facilitates confidence and growth.[31]

What Winnicott shows is that dependency and autonomy are not simply opposite terms, in tension. They certainly can be, as was the case for my aunt. It is not easy to reconcile taking away someone's independence and subverting their will because they need to be better cared for, and I remained plagued by doubt in the months that followed her admission to aged care. But I am also thinking of Anna's description of her role in the spinal cord injury unit, where she helps others in need, in order that they can realise their 'own goals in life'.

I am not suggesting that Winnicott's thinking neatly maps on to the scenarios scrutinised in this book. However, it is stimulating to work with his insights, in order to close by envisaging transformed and more humane relations between those needing help and the state's efforts to look after them. What might it mean if, in a period of dependency on welfare, the dependent being turned to the state and saw not the face of a disciplinarian, punitive figure, but instead a concern for them and their particular circumstances reflected back to them—'me as a whole person', as Lallie expressed it? I recorded one interview that gave me more concrete clues as to how nurturance might in turn foster autonomy and facilitate self-realisation.

∴

Shortly before Bec's first appointment with a ParentsNext provider, she had 'just been diagnosed with a medical condition'. She told me, 'And I don't identify as having a disability: just because I have a medical condition doesn't mean that I can't work.' Bec went into that first appointment, she relayed, with 'attitude'. She immediately asserted, 'Don't you ever view me as being disabled because I'm not. Because I can manage my medical condition.'

Her case manager's response surprised her: 'Well, actually I have the same medical condition as you. And I'm a case manager. And with your qualification that you're doing, you can have my job if you wanted it.' It was a funny moment, and the relationship evolved from there. 'She was an amazing case manager. And she—I think she had a similar background in some areas, and she could identify and resonate with some of my experiences.'

Bec was already studying, which became her agreed-upon participation activity. Her resolve was strong: 'After I left the DV [domestic violence] situation I made a promise to my children and myself that I was never going to be in that situation again.' That is, she was 'never going to be homeless again'.

Determination is one thing, life circumstances another. She dropped out of study because of ongoing abuse by her ex. At the point she was compulsorily required to commence ParentsNext, she had re-enrolled in a counselling diploma. This period of study was subject to further interruptions, but slowly she moved through it. The course content supported her healing. Bec also enrolled in other short courses with therapeutic and practical goals, rebuilding the networks she'd lost in leaving her youngest child's dad. Further, she volunteered facilitating a women's group.

Every time her ParentsNext appointment rolled around, 'I was the one steering it.' Bec continued, 'I was like, "I know what my goal is." And I shared it. Like, it was time-bound, it was realistic and it was achievable. And my case manager—she knew that I knew what I was doing. She knew that I was more than capable, and she let me steer in the direction that she knew I wanted to go.' Bec's case manger 'was like, "You've already created a goal for yourself. It's a pointless exercise me putting added pressure on you to do extra stuff."' In sum, they 'worked together'.

Bec's case manager eventually left the provider's employment. Before she moved on, they discussed who Bec would work with next. Bec chose a man I will call George, who was also 'amazing'. By this stage, she was a qualified counsellor and looking for work. She discussed a job application with him. George looked over Bec's CV and told her it was 'crap'. Bec started laughing. George and Bec then devoted the rest of the appointment to fixing her CV together: 'he actually sat there with me'.

George is a psychologist; Bec always found him 'good to talk to'. He was sympathetic about the anxiety associated with the reporting system and set up her app, talking her through it. Bec found both case managers 'genuine' and 'passionate'.

There is a lot to unpack here and a number of cautions to make. First, Bec insists she does not wish to be defined by her disability. For many, it is imperative that their diagnosis not so much defines them but is accepted as a legitimate reason they can't work. Securing access to the Disability Support Pension is extremely difficult and burdensome; without the more generous level of support, disabled and sick people languish on JobSeeker, are subject to harmful conditions and might not be able to afford the treatments they need.

This was not, however, Bec's story. Bec was in a position to narrate her self-understanding as someone who didn't want to be defined by or limited by her medical condition. Her life had been shaped by violence and homelessness in the past, but she sought to pursue future employment helping others in need. Not everyone is in this situation, and I am not suggesting that determination is the missing ingredient. Further, I am neither approving nor disapproving of Bec's decision to, in effect, drop the attitude. Another of my interviewees told me that she knew from experience that being an 'uppity poor person' was risky, but also conveyed to me that it eroded her self-respect to become a more docile supplicant.

What is significant about this story is that, in her case manager, Bec was invited to see a version of herself, as the case manager emphasised the 'resonances' between their circumstances. Later, George, who also listened to rather than directed Bec, referred to her CV as 'crap'. This might at first seem like an unprofessional insult. What Bec communicated through cadence and laughter, though, was that she did not hear or receive it as an insult. I didn't either. I heard respect in this story. That is, I grasped that George was being honest with Bec, rather than patronising her, or ticking a box and moving on. Her CV needed work: together, they undertook this work.

To be clear, I do not draw a practical lesson from Bec's experiences so much as a theoretical one. I have described ParentsNext as emblematic of punitive and conditional welfare delivery. I do not recommend 'fixing' or tweaking it through better case work. What I do see is this: Winnicott's notions are at play here, and they are worth teasing out.

Bec could not build a new life for herself alone: total independence is an utter fantasy, and she did not indulge it. She talked to me of the many supportive figures she had turned to as she created a new reality against a backdrop of poverty and ongoing stresses. A more caring welfare system could have provided support—such as housing—to alleviate the material pressures she was faced with. Bec did not receive such support, which made a hard situation harder. That is, the Australian welfare state did not provide adequate resources with which she could sustain and reproduce life; instead, she faced the stress of coping on inadequate earnings.

Nonetheless, her case managers eventually joined the cast of support figures. They did so because they presented a different face of welfare. They looked at her and saw her, with interest and with care. In their faces, she did not see the will to punish her or to 'tick boxes'. Bec saw instead a commitment both to understanding her story and a genuine offer to assist in her efforts to reauthor it.

Afterword

Who cares?

Late on the evening of 21 May 2022, Anthony Albanese took the stage to claim victory in the federal election. Albanese paid tribute to his mum, the late Maryanne Ellery, who raised him alone in inner-city public housing. Ellery suffered from rheumatoid arthritis, and her source of income was the Invalid Pension, an earlier iteration of today's Disability Support Pension. That night, Albanese felt his mum 'beaming down' on his election as prime minister.[1]

In a Twitter thread on Mother's Day the previous year, around twenty years after his mum's death, Albanese explained that their public housing 'gave us a sense of security and stability'. He continued, 'It was our home.' He also remembered that the 'cutbacks that happened in mum's lifetime meant she had to justify the support she was receiving'. Albanese stated, 'I know the difference that governments can make on people's lives because I lived it.'

I am not sure what specific cutbacks Albanese was referring to, or exactly the ways in which Maryanne Ellery needed to justify the ongoing support she was entitled to. What is clear is that the welfare state that Ellery and her only son depended upon in the 1960s and 1970s has been utterly transformed in the decades since Albanese came of age.

Albanese was born in 1963. In the mid-1960s, public housing represented 8 per cent of housing in Australia. Since then, public housing stock has been both sold off and neglected: less than 3 per cent of dwellings in Australia are public housing.[2] It has also become increasingly onerous and difficult to secure the Disability Support Pension, which is more generous than JobSeeker. Application success rates have fallen from 63 per cent in 2011 to 41 per cent in 2021.[3] This has seen many more people with disabilities assessed as having a 'partial capacity to work' and their income support payment receipt subject to conditions.

Perhaps, then, when Anthony Albanese was a toddler, his mum would have been required to participate in ParentsNext as a condition of receiving a social security payment. She might have had to report their weekly attendance at a local playgroup. And if she forgot to report one week, or if she ever had problems using the app, or if little Albo was sick that week, they might have found themselves depending on a neighbour's generosity for groceries or missing out on a crucial discount offered for a bill paid early. This is pure speculation, of course. But while Albanese has indisputably lived the effects of government policy in welfare recipients' lives and understands its capacity to care, he hasn't lived the effects of today's more stingy, conditional and quick-to-penalise welfare system. The people featured in these pages have.

In his victory speech, Albanese talked about looking after 'the disadvantaged and the vulnerable' as well as the importance of 'kindness to those in need'. Indeed, two sustained campaigns about the miserable unemployment rate, from 2011 to 2013 and 2018 to 2020, led by peak bodies and increasingly by anti-poverty activists, have been effective in generating increased public sympathy for those subsisting on JobSeeker, the income support payment for unemployed people.[4] Support for 'raising the rate' is now at 57 per cent, according to some polls.[5] This statistic is a direct answer to the bald question of 'Who cares?' Yet despite the shift in public opinion, both major parties have spent more than twenty years emphasising the dignity of waged work and have proved reluctant to lift unemployment benefits out of a 'concern that a more generous payment would provide disincentives to seek employment'.[6] Despite its caring rhetoric, then, the Albanese government has no plans to lift the JobSeeker rate. Can there be any more urgent exercise in looking after 'those in need'?

As to the cashless debit card, the Albanese government went to the election committed to abolishing the card. Rishworth moved swiftly, visiting Ceduna and the East Kimberley in June and soon after introducing legislation to abolish the card.

What does it mean, then, that this crudest manifestation of the conditional welfare state has been walked back? Does this represent a deeper shift in the conceptualisation of the contemporary welfare state's caring role, or is it more contained? An edging away from an unpalatable, expensive, race-based policy experiment, which two commissioned evaluations could not definitively establish had 'worked'? There are no prizes for the readers who have guessed it's the latter option. A mean-spirited, conditional and punitive welfare regime remains firmly in place.

As for ParentsNext, at the time of writing this program is unchanged, but pressure is mounting for its redesign, even abolition. I have represented ParentsNext, which affects mostly single mothers in receipt of Parenting Payment (Single), as a welfare reform measure that exemplifies the widening net of conditionality. Parents of babies as young as nine months old are subject to compulsory participation in this program. They are compelled to sign a 'participation plan', an instrument that commands often absurd commitments to undertake approved activities, such as when Megan enrolled in an online aromatherapy course to free herself from reporting requirements for a time.

Certainly, ParentsNext has emerged in this book as a much more ambiguous innovation than that of the cashless debit card. ParentsNext can be characterised—and indeed meaningfully experienced—as a supportive program, which assists parents on social security payments to find their way back into the workforce. Think of Lallie's upgraded Zoom account and Bec's empowering dialogue with successive supportive case managers. What could be wrong with that? It might even seem downright anti-feminist to critique a program geared towards supporting single mums' participation in the workforce. However, the provision of this support, which is by no means always forthcoming, is conditional on extensively monitored compliance. Fulfilling the digitised reporting conditions attached to ParentsNext was a source of considerable anxiety for many of my interviewees. 'I feel like I have a target on my back' was Trish's summing up. Furthermore a failure to report one's compliance correctly and on time results in payment suspensions—an abrupt loss of income that affects a parent and their child or children alike.

More broadly, ParentsNext sheds light on the gender dynamics of the contemporary welfare state. Whereas the twentieth-century welfare state rested on the figure of the white male 'breadwinner' and his dependants, the welfare state today deems parenting as non-productive and all forms of dependency pathological. Caring is delegitimised as inactivity, while the parents of infants are recast as essentially 'unemployed'. Like other unemployed persons, they are subject to chaotic and arbitrary governance of their circumstances. In the process, the role of parenting and the work it involves is erased and devalued.

As much as my ostensible focus has been these two welfare measures, I have also tried to see beyond the welfare state's uncaring policy architecture. I do not perceive or categorise the people I have interviewed in terms of the thing they were not currently doing when I encountered them, or at least were not doing full-time: paid work. Certainly, I had many conversations with welfare recipients about the paid jobs they had undertaken in the past or were doing then, while also being eligible for social security to supplement their earnings. I amassed a long list: aged care; childcare; packing hay bales; sifting, rummaging and salvaging at the tip. Real estate; therapist; accountant. Cleaning offices, and cleaning 'down the caravan park'. Easter bunny in a department store: 'Dressed up with the ears and the little white bobtail in the sweets section.' One single mum told me angrily that she worked at a bank for ten years before suffering a workplace injury. The bank's attitude was: 'Don't care; see you later; you can't do your job any more; bye.' Another interviewee was once a croupier and later a cobbler.

However, beyond many welfare recipients' extensive involvement in waged work, I also see people working hard to practise and undertake care; that of their own biological infants in most cases but also more widely distributed care in many others. Svetlana, a recovered drug addict and severely isolated single mum, who was homeless when she gave birth, talked of a raw determination to keep her only baby alive. Elsie, the Pitjantjatjara woman whose life stories I recorded for another book, was much more enmeshed in widely distributed and reciprocal relations of care, carefully listing the many community members she had had a hand in raising and checking the string of names with me many times in case she had neglected to mention anyone. I also recorded stories about looking after one's siblings as children and about nursing life partners and parents through periods of illness and as they died, as Gladys did so deliberately, methodically and lovingly.

In addition to the caregiving narrated to me, in this book I document gestures and practices that might seem minor but in fact were critical to stretching resources to sustain households, provide meals and cushion the harshest effects of living in poverty in an uncaring welfare state. These practices were also about finding ways to snatch flashes of pleasure as well as pride. I am thinking of the $50 directly debited from an utterly broke young Aboriginal man's bank account each fortnight and deposited onto his mum's electricity account. This man commented casually to me once, 'I got nothing this week.' He elaborated, 'On the off week, you can't even manage. It's real hard.' Yet he was committed to helping his mum out, claiming for himself an honourable social role in the process. I am also thinking of the box of groceries a friend dropped at Natasha's house when her payment was temporarily suspended and a story about the way $50 circulates between single mums in an online group, which provides solidarity and support. They joke it is the same $50 note, in endless motion.

Waged work is undoubtedly the primary source of identity in our society. Yet this book insists that there are other kinds of work constantly being undertaken, other efforts expended, even by those who are in receipt of welfare and not understood to be working. This labour ultimately creates people, relationships and feelings, rather than commodities and services. It is essential, and it's not going anywhere. In a low-carbon future, the work of care will prove enduring. Appreciating what it takes and all who do it will only become more critical.

Notes

Preface

1. Fisher and Tronto, 'Towards a feminist theory of caring', p. 40.
2. Boyer, *The Undying*, p. 107.
3. The additional $550 per fortnight was cut to $250 a fortnight in September 2020. The extra $250 per fortnight was paid until 31 December 2020, before dropping to a $150 fortnightly supplement, which was paid until the end of March 2021. ABC News, 'Jobseeker changes Coronavirus supplement reduction extension'.
4. ABC News, 'Jobseeker recipients in line for extra $25 a week'.
5. O'Connell and Coonan, 'The effects of Delta on the unemployed'.
6. Convery and Henriques-Gomes, '"We need to be alarmed": Food banks in overdrive as politicians allow Australians to go hungry'.

1 Look after them?

1. Mitchell, 'Negotiating vulnerability', p. 226.
2. *Social Security Legislation Amendment (Debit Card Trial) Act 2015*.
3. Data about the cashless debit card was released on a monthly basis. See 'Australian Government Cashless Debit Card Program'.
4. Australian Bureau of Statistics, 2016. See 'Quickstats' for the Ceduna (DC) Local Government Area and for Yalata.
5. Sheppard and Biddle, 'Class, capital and identity in Australian society', p. 506.
6. Eltham, 'A pandemic to die for'.
7. See 'Australian Government Cashless Debit Card Program'.
8. I gave driving lessons as part of the Learner Driver Mentor program, and am proud to have made a tiny contribution to this important program. For explanation of the way driving offences lead to fines, defaults and ultimately incarceration in remote Aboriginal Australia, see Grealy, 'Paperless arrests as preventative detention', p. 93.
9. Parliamentary Joint Committee on Human Rights, *ParentsNext*, p. 17; Community Affairs References Committee, *ParentsNext*, p. 3.
10. I use pseudonyms throughout this book except in the case of Ella, who requested that I use her real name.

11 Henriques-Gomes, 'Single parents forced to attend "story time" or lose Centrelink payments'; ABC News, 'ParentsNext program comes under fire from single mothers, who say it "makes life harder"'.
12 Community Affairs References Committee, *ParentsNext*.
13 Parliamentary Joint Committee on Human Rights, *ParentsNext*, p. 11.
14 Henriques-Gomes, 'ParentsNext'.
15 This term may be unfamiliar to some readers. I refer to a particular subset of colonial experience, whereby an invading society seeks to replace rather than only exploit the colonised peoples indigenous to the place. See Veracini, *Settler Colonialism*.
16 Illi, *Elsie Numitja Illi's Tjukurpa*, p. 4.
17 Swain and Trompf, 'Tradition', p. 32.
18 Illi, *Elsie Numitja Illi's Tjukurpa*, p. 4.
19 Buchanan, *Ko Taranaki te Maunga*, p. 12.
20 O'Sullivan, McGann and Considine, *Buying and Selling the Poor*, p. 11.
21 A vast literature analyses this global shift. For example, Mounk, *The Age of Responsibility*.
22 Schram et al., 'Deciding to discipline', pp. 398–9.
23 Alston, *Digital Technology, Social Protection and Human Rights*, p. 17. The specific examples in this paragraph are all drawn from Alston's report. For more in-depth consideration of the workings of digitised welfare systems, see Eubanks, *Automating Inequality*, and Fowkes, 'Seeing people in the computer'.
24 O'Sullivan, McGann and Considine, *Buying and Selling the Poor*, p. 11.
25 Bryson and Verity, 'Australia'.
26 Senate Estimates Hansard, Community Affairs Legislation Committee, Tuesday, 7 April 2022, p. 10.
27 Dickinson, *Feeding the Crisis*, pp. 12–13.
28 Burns, 'Whistleblowers say some employment service providers are exploiting the ParentsNext welfare scheme'.
29 For key texts examining the historical context, ideological dimensions and genealogy of conditional welfare in Australia, see Beilharz, Considine and Watts, *Arguing about the Welfare State*; Carney and Ramia, 'Mutuality, Mead and McClure'; Taylor, Gray and Stanton, 'New conditionality in Australian social security policy'; Marston, 'The war on the poor'; Mendes, *Empowerment and Control in the Australian Welfare State*. For important work centred on welfare recipients' experiences of welfare conditionality, see Casey, '"Job Seeker" experiences of punitive activation in Job Services Australia'; Casey, 'Single mothers and resistance to welfare-to-work'; Mitchell, 'Negotiating vulnerability'; Mitchell, *Making a Life on Mean Welfare*; Murphy et al., *Half a Citizen*; Peterie et al., 'Emotional compliance

and emotion as resistance'; Soldatić et al., 'Emplacing indigeneity and rurality in neoliberal disability welfare reform'.
30 See also Mitchell, *Making a Life on Mean Welfare*.
31 Fisher and Tronto, 'Towards a feminist theory of caring', p. 40.
32 Fennell, 'The family toxic', pp. 14, 21.
33 Whittaker, *Blakwork*, p. 148.
34 Anthropologist Catherine Fennell describes a similar dynamic within her research with public housing residents in Chicago. Formal interviews made people feel like they were, once again, being scrutinised to determine their eligibility for benefits. I am guided by Fennell's reflections on what readers expect from an account of the lives of marginalised strangers—information and intimacy—and her reluctance to fulfil these expectations. Fennell, *Last Project Standing*, pp. 61–3.
35 Jackson, 'Introduction', p. 22.
36 'Painful porosity' is a term adopted from psychoanalyst Alison Clark's exploration of why analysts and writers do what they do. I think Clark's analysis might also be productively applied to the practice of anthropology. Clark, 'Unconscious choice', p. 712.
37 Hill and Carroll, 'Australia's national tobacco campaign'.
38 Cooper, 'Money as punishment'.
39 Warin et al., 'Short horizons and obesity futures'.
40 Tumarkin, *Axiomatic*, p. 89.
41 See Gregg, *Counterproductive*.
42 Graeber, 'After the pandemic, we can't go back to sleep'.

2 Sustenance

1 Irish, *Hidden in Plain View*, p. 35.
2 See Symons, *One Continuous Picnic*.
3 Brundage, *The English Poor Laws*.
4 Linebaugh, *The London Hanged*, p. 13.
5 Dickey, 'Why were there no poor laws in Australia?'
6 See Murphy, 'The pauper in the new world', in *A Decent Provision*, pp. 7–28.
7 O'Brien, 'Creating the Aboriginal pauper', p. 11.
8 Norman, 'Parramatta and Black Town Native Institutions'.
9 O'Brien, 'Creating the Aboriginal pauper', p. 16.
10 Ibid., p. 18.
11 Gapps, 'Strike them with terror', p. 143.
12 Morris, *Domesticating Resistance*, p. 6.
13 O'Brien, 'Kitchen fragments and garden stuff', p. 163.
14 See McGregor, *Imagined Destinies*.

15 Murphy, *A Decent Provision*, p. 66.
16 Ibid., p. 77.
17 Harris, 'Penny-pinching activities', pp. 288–9.
18 Murphy, *A Decent Provision*, p. 69.
19 Ibid., p. 68.
20 Ibid., p. 68.
21 Ibid., p. 87.
22 Castles, 'Needs-based strategies of social protection in Australia and New Zealand', p. 93.
23 Ibid.
24 Swain, 'Writing the history of women and welfare', p. 44.
25 Park, *Swords and Crowns and Rings*, pp. 388–9.
26 Harris, 'From relief to mutual obligation', p. 9.
27 Ibid., p. 10.
28 Beaumont, *Australia's Great Depression*, p. 239.
29 Harris, 'From relief to mutual obligation', pp. 10–11.
30 Watts, 'The origins of the Australian welfare state', p. 240. One of the key points Watts makes is that the twentieth-century welfare state, which was consolidated under the post-war Chifley government, is not the Labor Party's legacy alone.
31 Harris, 'From relief to mutual obligation', p. 14.
32 Murphy, *A Decent Provision*, p. 203.
33 Harris, 'From relief to mutual obligation', p. 11.
34 Ibid., p. 12.
35 Watts, 'The origins of the Australian welfare state', p. 228.
36 The literature about assimilation policies and the devastation they wrought is vast. See, for example, Haebich, *Broken Circles*.
37 Exclusion is emphasised in Altman and Sanders, 'From exclusion to dependence', and in Cass, 'Contested debates about citizenship rights to welfare'.
38 Altman and Sanders, 'From exclusion to dependence', p. 208.
39 Ibid., p. 209.
40 Murphy, 'Conditional inclusion'.
41 McGrath, 'Beneath the skin', p. 105.
42 Ibid., p. 105.
43 Altman and Saunders, 'From exclusion to dependence', p. 209.
44 Skyring, 'Low wages, low rents and pension cheques'. See also Jebb, *Blood, Sweat and Welfare*, pp. 255–76.
45 Murphy, 'Conditional inclusion', p. 225.
46 White, 'Peas, beans and riverbanks'.
47 Beckett, 'From island to mainland'.

48 Young, 'Dingo scalping and the frontier economy'.
49 The phrase is Max Weber's: Weber, *The Protestant Ethic and the Spirit of Capitalism*, p. 179.
50 Young, 'Dingo scalping and the frontier economy', p. 101.
51 Illi, *Elsie Numitja Illi's Tjukurpa*, p. 14.
52 Norman, 'Aboriginal worlds and Australian capitalism', p. 68.
53 Brock, 'Pastoral stations and reserves in South and Central Australia', p. 111.
54 Morris, 'From underemployment to unemployment'.

3 Surveillance

1   Maguire, *This is What a Feminist Looks Like*, p. 126.
2   Humphrys, *How Labour Built Neoliberalism*, pp. 77–8.
3   Mendes, *Empowerment and Control in the Australian Welfare State*, p. 68.
4   Harvey, *A Brief History of Neoliberalism*, p. 3.
5   Ayesha also asked me, 'from one mum to another', the key question surrounding the juggling of work demands and parenting: 'Do you feel guilty?' My reply? 'Constantly.' Later I realised that guilt was not quite the right word. I feel unresolved about it.
6   Archer, 'Dole bludgers, tax payers and the New Right'.
7   See Murphy et al., *Half a Citizen*, pp. 3, 90, 167.
8   Mead, 'Welfare reform and the family'.
9   Mead, 'The rise of paternalism'.
10 Cooper, *Family Values*.
11 Kingfisher and Goldsmith, 'Reforming women in the United States and Aotearoa/New Zealand', p. 714. For analysis of Australian political debates about 'dependency', see Mendes, *Empowerment and Control in the Australian Welfare State*, p. 158.
12 Considine, *Enterprising States*; McGann, Nguyen and Considine, 'Welfare conditionality and blaming the unemployed', p. 469.
13 O'Sullivan, McGann and Considine, *Buying and Selling the Poor*, p. 13.
14 Mendes, *Empowerment and Control in the Australian Welfare State*, p. 146. For illuminating analysis of Howard-era debates about welfare receipt, see Soldatić and Pini, 'The three Ds of welfare reform'.
15 Bessant, 'Regulating the unemployed', p. 80. For discussion of safety concerns associated with Work for the Dole, see O'Sullivan, McGann and Considine, *Buying and Selling the Poor*, p. 33.
16 Fowkes, *The Application of Income Support Obligations and Penalties to Remote Indigenous Australians*, p. 19.
17 Yeatman, 'Mutual obligation'.
18 Mauss, *The Gift*.

19 Marston and McDonald, 'Feeling motivated yet?', p. 263.
20 O'Sullivan, McGann and Considine, *Buying and Selling the Poor*, p. 192.
21 McGann, Nguyen and Considine, 'Welfare conditionality and blaming the unemployed'. For further discussion see O'Sullivan, McGann and Considine, *Buying and Selling the Poor*, pp. 19, 121, 141, 173–4.
22 Adkins, 'Disobedient workers, the law and the making of unemployment markets', p. 300.
23 Mitchell, *Making a Life on Mean Welfare*.
24 Cooper, *Family Values*.
25 Wacquant, *Punishing the Poor*. American welfare spending itself has not shrunk since 1996. Instead, Dickinson shows that America's social safety net has been essentially retooled to underwrite low-wage precarious labour: welfare, in the form of food stamps, supplements inadequate wages, while the unemployed subsist on charitable food pantries. Dickinson, *Feeding the Crisis*.
26 See McKenzie, *Getting By*, and Beresford, *All Our Welfare*.
27 Curchin, Weight and Ritter, 'Moral framings in the Australian parliamentary debate on drug testing of welfare recipients'.
28 Gredley, 'Government "knew Robodebt was illegal": Emails'.
29 For a collation of personal Robodebt stories, see notmydebt.com.au. McKenzie-Murray, 'Centrelink's debt collection "pushed him over the edge"'.
30 Whiteford, 'Robodebt was a policy fiasco'.
31 Spies-Butcher, 'Marketisation and the dual welfare state', p. 197.
32 Rothwell, 'Indigenous insiders chart an end to victimhood', pp. 15, 16.
33 Pearson, 'Passive welfare and the destruction of Indigenous society in Australia'.
34 Pearson, 'Our right to take responsibility', p. 143.
35 Ibid., p. 155.
36 Rowse, 'McClure's "mutual obligation" and Pearson's "reciprocity"'.
37 Martin, *Is Welfare Dependency 'Welfare Poison'?*, p. 20.
38 Watt, 'Pearson's mission', p. 45.
39 Silverstein and McLisky, 'Rethinking paternalism', pp. 41, 46.
40 Pascoe, *Dark Emu*.
41 Povinelli, *Labor's Lot*.
42 Altman and Johns, *Indigenous Welfare Reform in the Northern Territory and Cape York*.
43 Ibid., p. 12.
44 Gray and Bray, 'ANU Centre for Social Methods and Research submission into Social Security (Administration) Amendment (Income Management and Cashless Welfare) Bill 2019', p. 2.

45	Data about the BasicsCard is released on a monthly basis. See 'Australian Government Income Management Program'.
46	Needham, 'Sunbelt imperialism', p. 244.
47	Ellem, *The Pilbara*, p. 162.
48	Cleary, *Title Fight*, p. 60.
49	Ibid., p. 42.
50	Detailed accounts of these meetings are found in ibid., pp. 80–5, 158–63.
51	See Scambary, *My Country, Mine Country*. Paul Cleary notes that Aboriginal people comprise 10 per cent of FMG's workforce and that FMG also 'claims to have awarded more than $2 billion worth of contracts to businesses run by traditional owners in the Pilbara'. Both sets of figures, Cleary notes, are 'unaudited'. Cleary, *Title Fight*, p. 61.
52	Forrest, *The Forrest Review*, p. 28.
53	Klein and Razi, 'Contemporary tools of dispossession', p. 89.
54	See 'Australian Government Cashless Debit Card Program'. See also Mavromaras et al., *Cashless Debit Card Baseline Data Collection in the Goldfields Region*, for more detailed background on this region.
55	Marston et al., *Hidden Costs*, p. 99.
56	Senate Hansard, Tuesday, 8 December 2020, p. 7027.
57	Henriques-Gomes and Murphy, 'Cashless debit card extended for two years after Senate rejects plan to make it permanent'.

4 'Stressed out to be on the card'

1	Dalley, 'The "white card" is grey', pp. 52, 54.
2	Klein and Razi, *The Cashless Debit Card Trial in the East Kimberley*, p. 13.
3	Binks, 'Optimism over card trial'.
4	ABC News, 'Cashless welfare card to be trialled in South Australia region next year'.
5	Hinkson and Vincent, 'Shifting Indigenous Australian realities'.
6	Lea, *Wild Policy*.
7	Mendes, 'Top-down paternalism versus bottom-up community development', pp. 50, 52.
8	Megalogenis, 'Australasia rising'.
9	Binks, 'Protestors voice concerns'.
10	Massola, 'Malcolm Turnbull flags national roll-out of cashless welfare card, met by protests'.
11	*Social Security (Administration) Amendment (Continuation of Cashless Welfare) Act 2020*.
12	Francis Markham made this point at a forum discussing the *Remote Access* report. See Staines et al., *Remote Access*.

13	For an important account of one community's determined efforts to tackle alcohol's impact in this region, see Brady, Byrne and Henderson, 'Which bloke would stand up for Yalata?'. Wright's electrifying *Grog War* provides a detailed account of the way the Julalikari Council forced changes to alcohol availability in the Northern Territory town of Tennant Creek in the mid-1990s and the formidable opposition mounted by licensees. Throughout the process, Julalikari emphasised that alcohol abuse affected the whole community and demanded a whole-of-community response.
14	Mbembe, 'Necropolitics', pp. 22–3.
15	Pearson, 'Tony Abbott and the white man's burden'.
16	AAP Factcheck, 'Cashless welfare cost is way off the money'.
17	ABC News, 'Centrelink cashless welfare card trial costing taxpayers $10 000 per participant'.
18	Dalley, 'The "white card" is grey', p. 57.
19	ORIMA Research, *Cashless Debit Card Trial Evaluation*, p. 6.
20	See Holderhead, 'NXT hit on Ceduna's card trial'.
21	House of Representatives Hansard, Monday, 5 February 2018, p. 172.
22	Exemptions from Cashless Debit Card Program, Department of Social Services.
23	Peterie, Marston and Humpage, 'The trope of the vulnerable child in conditional welfare discourses'. See also Irene Watson, 'In the Northern Territory intervention, what is saved or rescued and at what cost?'; Nicole Watson, 'The Northern Territory Emergency Response'.
24	McCutcheon, 'Is the cashless debit card working?'
25	ORIMA Research, *Cashless Debit Card Trial Evaluation*, p. 7.
26	See Hunt, 'The cashless debit card evaluation'. Other objections to the ORIMA report were less convincing to me. Sociologist Eva Cox posited that the evaluation raised serious 'ethical questions' because it involved asking Aboriginal people about things they might find distressing. Although her comment was well meaning, it relies on the very image of Indigenous incapacity that the card is meant to address: Indigenous people are again cast as primarily damaged, vulnerable and in need of protection. Cox, 'Submission into Senate Standing Committee on Community Affairs, Social Services Legislation Amendment (Cashless Debit Card) Bill 2017', p. 8.
27	Australian National Audit Office, *The Implementation and Performance of the Cashless Debit Card*, p. 8.
28	Greenacre et al., 'Income management of government payments on welfare', p. 9.
29	Marston et al., *Hidden Costs*, p. 122.
30	Mavromaras et al., *Evaluation of the Cashless Debit Card in Ceduna, East Kimberley and the Goldfields Region*, p. 2.

31 Tudge, 'Additional services for Ceduna as part of welfare card trial'.
32 Australian National Audit Office, *Implementation and Performance of the Cashless Debit Card—Follow-On*, p. 56.
33 Ibid., pp. 10, 60.
34 ABC News, 'Cashless debit card trial to end with auditor-general's report the final nail in its coffin'.
35 *Social Security (Administration) Amendment (Repeal of Cashless Debit Card and Other Measures) Act 2022*.
36 Galloway, 'Government to create new welfare card to phase out Howard era Basics Card'.

5 'Why are you crying? We're here to help you'

1 Services Australia, 'ParentsNext'.
2 See Flanagan, 'Imagine us as part of you'.
3 Macauley, *Simpson Returns*, pp. 1, 15.
4 www.abs.gov.au/statistics/labour/employment-and-unemployment/labour-force-status-families/latest-release#one-parent-families
5 Davidson et al., *Poverty in Australia, 2018*, p. 40.
6 Brady, 'Researching governmentalities through ethnography', p. 268.
7 Casey, 'Single mothers and resistance to welfare-to-work', p. 6.
8 Brady, 'Researching governmentalities through ethnography', p. 276.
9 Casey, 'Single mothers and resistance to welfare-to-work', p. 6.
10 Gerrard and Farrugia, 'Workers in waiting?'
11 Community Affairs References Committee, *ParentsNext*, p. 4.
12 Ibid., p. 29. For close examination of the relationship between ParentsNext and Aboriginal women's care labour, see Klein, 'Unpaid care, welfare conditionality and expropriation'.
13 Parliamentary Joint Committee on Human Rights, *ParentsNext*, p. 9.
14 Ibid., p. 66.
15 Cash, Letter to Chair, Parliamentary Joint Committee on Human Rights, p. 2.
16 Malcolm, *The Silent Woman*, p. 183.
17 Adkins, 'Out of work', p. 159.
18 Brady, 'Researching governmentalities through ethnography', p. 264.
19 O'Sullivan, McGann and Considine, *Buying and Selling the Poor*, p. 77.
20 Ibid., pp. 183–4.
21 Nguyen and Velayutham, 'Street-level discretion, emotional labour and welfare frontline staff'.
22 Ibid.
23 McGann, Nguyen and Considine, 'Welfare conditionality and blaming the unemployed'.

24	I had an interesting conversation with Jo about her foster caring. I sought to validate this caring work and commented that fostering was a kind of 'job'. She corrected me warmly: 'It's a vocation. Something you believe in.'
25	Sennett and Cobb, *The Hidden Injuries of Class*, p. 191.
26	Shildrick and MacDonald, 'Poverty talk', p. 291.
27	Patrick, 'Living with and responding to the "scrounger" narrative'.
28	'Social security payments—Residence criteria'.
29	McRobbie, *Feminism and the Politics of Resilience*, p. 101.
30	For analysis of the raced work undertaken at the bottom of the supply chain, see Stead, 'Precarity's reach'.
31	Soldatić et al., *Dead Ends*, p. 13.
32	Peel, *The Lowest Rung*, p. 95.

6 'They think we're rubbish'

1	Bennett, 'The 1967 referendum', p. 29.
2	Sennett, *Respect in a World of Inequality*, p. 117.
3	Mitchell and Vincent, 'The shame of welfare?'
4	Biddle, 'Shame', p. 236.
5	Sennett, *Respect in a World of Inequality*, p. 12.
6	Ibid., p. 3.
7	Weber, 'Bureaucracy', p. 51.
8	https://data.gov.au/data/dataset/australian-government-cashless-debit-card-program
9	Ibid.
10	Department of Social Services, 'Ceduna Community Panel'.
11	Graeber, 'Dead zones of the imagination', p. 108.
12	Lea, 'From little things, big things grow'.
13	The application form was available from Department of Social Services, 'Ceduna Community Panel'.
14	Myers, *Pintupi Country, Pintupi Self*.
15	Arthur, *Aboriginal English*, p. 107.
16	Ibid., pp. 107–8.
17	Baak, 'Transnational families, remittances, cieng and obligation for Dinka women in Australia', p. 126.
18	McCormack, 'Resisting the welfare mother', p. 361.
19	Ibid., p. 371.
20	Ibid., p. 373.
21	Watt, 'Is the BasicsCard "shaming" Aboriginal people?'
22	Dalley, 'The "white card" is grey', p. 56.

7 'Had to be done'

1. Vuong, *On Earth We're Briefly Gorgeous*, p. 91.
2. Ehrenreich, *Nickel and Dimed*, pp. 116, 117.
3. Wynhausen, *Dirt Cheap*, p. 96.
4. Fisher and Tronto, 'Towards a feminist theory of caring', p. 40.
5. Marston et al., *Compulsory Income Management in Australia and New Zealand*, p. 77.
6. See also O'Sullivan, McGann and Considine, *Buying and Selling the Poor*, p. 135, for one of many examples in this book of employment service agencies claiming outcomes for jobs they played no part in helping their clients secure.
7. This was an authorised letter to residents by Tony Burke, MP, Member for Watson, dropped into letterboxes as part of the 2022 federal election campaign.
8. Meagher, 'A genealogy of aged care'. Migrants also make up a significant and growing proportion of this workforce. According to the 2016 Census, 50 per cent of personal care assistants and 37 per cent of aged-care and disability workers were born overseas. Workers from non-English-speaking backgrounds are more susceptible to casual employment and underemployment. Charlesworth and Isherwood, 'Migrant aged-care workers in Australia', p. 2704.
9. Fisher and Tronto, 'Towards a feminist theory of caring', p. 44.
10. Cooper, *Family Values*, p. 53.
11. For example, Mendes, *Empowerment and Control in the Australian Welfare State*, pp. 155–8. For a comprehensive overview of the literature see Arthur, 'Welfare dependency'.
12. Fraser and Gordon, 'A genealogy of dependency', p. 313.
13. Ibid., p. 314.
14. Ibid., p. 315.
15. Ibid., p. 318.
16. Ibid., p. 323.
17. Sennett, *Respect in a World of Inequality*, p. 107.
18. Taylor, *The Last Asylum*, p. 162.
19. Ibid., p. 248.
20. Ibid., p. 248.
21. Simmonds, 'Troubled minds'.
22. Peterie, Marston and Humpage, 'The trope of the vulnerable child in conditional welfare discourses', p. 11.
23. See Peterson, 'Demand sharing', and Altman, 'A genealogy of "demand sharing"'.

24 Adkins, 'Out of work', p. 157. For a descriptive account of the amount of work and time involved in dealing with Centrelink see Murphy et al., *Half a Citizen*, pp. 138–64.
25 Cusk, *A Life's Work*, pp. 140, 141.
26 Soldatić, 'Appointment time', pp. 410, 411.
27 Parliamentary Joint Committee on Human Rights, *ParentsNext*, p. 9.
28 Soldatić, 'Appointment time', p. 414.
29 Anonymous submission into Senate Community Affairs References Committee inquiry into ParentsNext, including its trial and subsequent broader rollout (Submission no. 45), pp. 1, 2.
30 Winnicott, 'Mirror-role of mother and family in child development', in *Playing and Reality*.
31 Winnicott, 'The capacity to be alone', in *The Maturational Processes and the Facilitating Environment*.

Afterword: Who cares?

1 Albanese's victory speech is available in full via YouTube.
2 Pedestrian TV, 'Anti-poverty advocates say Albanese's childhood rhetoric is "cruel"'.
3 Soldatić et al., *Dead Ends*, p. 6.
4 See Mendes, 'Conditionalising the unemployed'.
5 This figure is derived from an Essential Poll, which asked respondents about the doubling of the unemployment rate as an emergency COVID-19 measure. In May 2020, 24 per cent of respondents thought the new rate of $560 per week should be maintained beyond the emergency measure's expiry date, and 33 per cent thought the former rate should be increased in line with the single pension to $472 per week. See Essential Report, 'Raising Newstart'.
6 Mendes, 'Conditionalising the unemployed', p. 44.

References

Legislation, reports and submissions

Alston, Philip. 2019. *Digital Technology, Social Protection and Human Rights*. Report of the Special Rapporteur on Extreme Poverty and Human Rights, United Nations General Assembly

Australian National Audit Office. 2018. *The Implementation and Performance of the Cashless Debit Card*. Commonwealth of Australia, Canberra

—2022. *Implementation and Performance of the Cashless Debit Card—Follow-On*. Commonwealth of Australia, Canberra

Cash, Michaelia. 2021. Letter to the Chair, Parliamentary Joint Committee on Human Rights. ParentsNext: Examination of Social Security (Parenting Payment Participation Requirements—Class of Persons) Instrument

Community Affairs References Committee. 2019. *ParentsNext, Including Its Trial and Subsequent Broader Rollout*. Commonwealth of Australia, Canberra

Cox, Eva. 2017. 'Submission into Senate Standing Committee on Community Affairs, Social Services Legislation Amendment (Cashless Debit Card) Bill 2017.' Submission no. 49

Davidson, Peter, Peter Saunders, Bruce Bradbury and Melissa Wong. 2018. *Poverty in Australia, 2018*. ACOSS/UNSW Poverty and Inequality Partnership Report No. 2. Australian Council of Social Services, Sydney

Forrest, Andrew. 2014. *The Forrest Review: Creating Parity*. Commonwealth of Australia, Canberra

Gray, Mathew, and Rob Bray. 2019. 'ANU Centre for Social Methods and Research Submission into Senate Standing Committee on Community Affairs, Social Security (Administration) Amendment (Income Management and Cashless Welfare) Bill 2019.' Submission no. 7

Hunt, Janet. 2017. *The Cashless Debit Card Evaluation: Does It Really Prove Success?* Centre for Aboriginal Economic Policy Research, Issue Paper no. 2. Australian National University, Canberra

Marston, Greg, Philip Mendes, Shelley Bielefeld, Michelle Peterie, Zoe Staines and Steven Roche. 2020. *Hidden Costs: An Independent Study into Income Management in Australia*. School of Social Science, University of Queensland, Brisbane

Mavromaras, Kostas, Megan Moskos, Linda Isherwood and Stéphane Mahutae. 2019. *Cashless Debit Card Baseline Data Collection in the Goldfields Region: Qualitative Findings*. Future of Employment and Skills Research Centre, University of Adelaide, Adelaide

Mavromaras, Kostas, Megan Moskos, Stéphane Mahutae and Linda Isherwood. 2021. *Evaluation of the Cashless Debit Card in Ceduna, East Kimberley and the Goldfields Region*. Future of Employment and Skills Research Centre, University of Adelaide, Adelaide

ORIMA Research. 2017. *Cashless Debit Card Trial Evaluation: Final Evaluation Report*. Australian Government, Department of Social Services, Melbourne

Parliamentary Joint Committee on Human Rights. 2021. *ParentsNext: Examination of Social Security (Parenting Payment Participation Requirements—Class of Persons) Instrument*. Commonwealth of Australia, Canberra

Social Security (Administration) Amendment (Continuation of Cashless Welfare) Act 2020

Social Security (Administration) Amendment (Repeal of Cashless Debit Card and Other Measures) Act 2022

Social Security Legislation Amendment (Debit Card Trial) Act 2015

Soldatić, Karen, Dina Bowman, Maria Mupanemunda and Patrick McGee. 2021. *Dead Ends: How Our Social Security System Is Failing People with Partial Capacity to Work*. Brotherhood of St Laurence, Fitzroy, Vic

Staines, Zoe, Jon Altman, Elise Klein and Francis Markham. 2021. *Remote Access: Guiding Principles for a New Livelihood and Work Program in Remote Indigenous Australia*. Australia Institute, Canberra

News stories and media releases

AAP Factcheck. 2021. 'Cashless welfare cost is way off the money.' 17 November.

ABC News. 2015. 'Cashless welfare card to be trialled in South Australia region next year.' 5 August.

—2017. 'Centrelink cashless welfare card trial costing taxpayers $10000 per participant.' 2 May.

—2019. 'ParentsNext program comes under fire from single mothers who say it "makes life harder".'

—2020. 'Jobseeker changes Coronavirus supplement reduction extension.' 10 November.

—2021. 'Jobseeker recipients in line for extra $25 a week.' 23 February.

—2022. 'Cashless debit card trial to end with auditor-general's report the final nail in its coffin.' 8 June.

Binks, Vanessa. 2015. 'Optimism over card trial.' *West Coast Sentinel*, 12 August.

—2015. 'Protestors voice concerns over welfare debit card trial.' *West Coast Sentinel*, 23 November.

Burns, Andy. 2019. 'Whistleblowers say some employment service providers are exploiting the ParentsNext welfare scheme.' 'Background Briefing', ABC News, 2 August.

Convery, Stephanie, and Luke Henriques-Gomes. 2021. '"We need to be alarmed": Food banks in overdrive as politicians allow Australians to go hungry.' *Guardian*, 21 November.

Galloway, Anthony. 2022. 'Government to create new welfare card to phase out Howard-era Basics Card'. *Sydney Morning Herald*, 9 October.

Gredley, Rebecca. 2020. 'Government "knew Robodebt was illegal": Emails.' *Australian Financial Review*, 6 February.

—2021. 'Cashless welfare card program costs $70m.' *West Australian*, 25 March.

Henriques-Gomes, Luke. 2018. 'Single parents forced to attend "story time" or lose Centrelink payments.' *Guardian*, 6 November.

—2019. 'ParentsNext: 80 per cent of recipients who had payments suspended not at fault, data shows.' *Guardian*, 15 September.

Henriques-Gomes, Luke, and Katharine Murphy. 2020. 'Cashless debit card extended for two years after Senate rejects plan to make it permanent.' *Guardian*, 10 December.

Holderhead, Sheradyn. 2018. 'NXT hit on Ceduna's card trial.' *Advertiser*, 9 February, p. 19

McCutcheon, Peter. 2020. 'Is the cashless debit card working?' *7.30*, 9 February.

McKenzie-Murray, Martin. 2017. 'Centrelink's debt collection "pushed him over the edge".' *Saturday Paper*, 18 February.

Massola, James. 2016. 'Malcolm Turnbull flags national roll-out of cashless welfare card, met by protests.' *Sydney Morning Herald*, 31 October.

Pedestrian TV. 2022. 'Anti-poverty advocates say Albanese's childhood rhetoric is "cruel" when he won't raise JobSeeker.' 1 June.

Tudge, Alan. 2015. 'Additional services for Ceduna as part of welfare card trial' (media release). Department of Prime Minister and Cabinet, 8 October.

Whiteford, Peter. 2020. 'Robodebt was a policy fiasco with a human cost we have yet to fully appreciate.' Probono Australia, 17 November.

Websites

Australian Bureau of Statistics

Data.gov.au, 'Australian Government Cashless Debit Card Program'.

Data.gov.au, 'Australian Government Income Management Program'.

Department of Social Services, 'Ceduna Community Panel'.

Department of Social Services, 'Exemptions from Cashless Debit Card Program'.

Department of Social Services, 'Social Security Payments—Residence Criteria'.

Essential Report, 2020. 'Raising Newstart', 5 May.

Hansard—Parliament of Australia.

Services Australia, 'ParentsNext'.

Other references

Adkins, Lisa. 2017. 'Disobedient workers, the law and the making of unemployment markets.' *Sociology*, 51(2):290–305

—2018. 'Out of work.' In *The Time of Money*, pp. 131–61. Stanford University Press, Stanford

Altman, Jon. 2011. 'A genealogy of "demand sharing": From pure anthropology to public policy.' In Yasmine Musharbash and Marcus Barber (eds), *Ethnography and the Production of Anthropological Knowledge: Essays in Honour of Nicolas Peterson*, pp. 187–200. ANU E-Press, Canberra

Altman, Jon, and Melissa Johns. 2008. *Indigenous Welfare Reform in the Northern Territory and Cape York: A Comparative Analysis*. Centre for Aboriginal Economic Policy Research, Canberra

Altman, Jon, and Will Sanders. 1995. 'From exclusion to dependence: Aborigines and the welfare state in Australia.' In John Dixon and Robert Scheurell (eds), *Social Welfare with Indigenous Peoples*, pp. 206–29. Routledge, London and New York

Archer, Verity. 2009. 'Dole bludgers, tax payers and the New Right: Constructing discourses of welfare in 1970s Australia.' *Labour History*, 96:177–90

Arthur, Don. 2021. 'Welfare dependency: The history of an idea.' Parliamentary Library Research Paper Series. Parliament of Australia, Canberra

Arthur, Jay. 1996. *Aboriginal English*. Oxford University Press, Melbourne

Baak, Melanie. 2015. 'Transnational families, remittances, cieng and obligation for Dinka women in Australia.' *Emotion, Space and Society*, 16:123–9

Beaumont, Joan. 2022. *Australia's Great Depression*. Allen & Unwin, Sydney

Beckett, Jeremy. 2010. 'From island to mainland: Torres Strait Islanders in the Australian labour force.' In Ian Keen (ed.), *Indigenous Participation in Australian Economies: Historical and Anthropological Perspectives*, pp. 63–72. ANU Press, Canberra

Beilharz, Peter, Mark Considine and Rob Watts (eds). 1992. *Arguing about the Welfare State: The Australian Experience*. Allen & Unwin, Sydney

Bennett, Scott. 1985. 'The 1967 referendum.' *Australian Aboriginal Studies*, 2:26–31

Beresford, Peter. 2016. *All Our Welfare: Towards Participatory Social Policy*. Policy Press, Bristol

Bessant, Judith. 2000. 'Regulating the unemployed: Australia's work-for-the-dole scheme.' *Journal of Australian Studies*, 24(64):75–84

Biddle, Jennifer. 1997. 'Shame.' *Australian Feminist Studies*, 12(26):227–39

Boyer, Anne. 2019. *The Undying: A Meditation on Modern Illness*. Penguin Random House, United Kingdom

Brady, Maggie, Joe Byrne and Graham Henderson. 2003. '"Which bloke would stand up for Yalata?": The struggle of an Aboriginal community to control the availability of alcohol.' *Australian Aboriginal Studies*, 2:62–71

Brady, Michelle. 2011. 'Researching governmentalities through ethnography: The case of Australian welfare reforms and programs for single parents.' *Critical Policy Studies*, 5(3):264–82

Brock, Peggy. 1995. 'Pastoral stations and reserves in South and Central Australia, 1850s–1950s.' In Ann McGrath and Kay Saunders (eds) with Jackie Huggins, *Aboriginal Workers*, pp. 102–14. Australian Society for the Study of Labour History, Sydney

Brundage, Anthony. 2022. *The English Poor Laws, 1700–1930*. Bloomsbury, United Kingdom

Bryson, Lois, and Fiona Verity. 2009. 'Australia: From wage-earners to neo-liberal welfare state.' In Pete Alcock and Gary Craig (eds), *International Social Policy: Welfare Regimes in the Developed World*, pp. 66–87. Palgrave Macmillan, Basingstoke

Buchanan, Rachel. 2018. *Ko Taranaki te Maunga*. Bridget Williams Books, Wellington, New Zealand

Carney, Terry, and Gaby Ramia. 2002. 'Mutuality, Mead and McClure: More "big Ms" for the unemployed.' *Australian Journal of Social Issues*, 37(3):277–300

Casey, Simone. 2020. '"Job Seeker" experiences of punitive activation in Job Services Australia.' *Australian Journal of Social Issues*. Online first

—2021. 'Single mothers and resistance to welfare-to-work: A Bourdieusian account.' *Journal of Sociology*. Online first

Cass, Bettina. 1995. 'Contested debates about citizenship rights to welfare: Indigenous people and welfare in Australia.' In Diane Austin-Broos and Gaynor Macdonald (eds), *Culture, Economy and Governance in Aboriginal Australia*, pp. 95–108. Sydney University Press, Sydney

Castles, Francis. 1996. 'Needs-based strategies of social protection in Australia and New Zealand.' In Gosta Esping-Andersen (ed.), *Welfare States in Transition*, pp. 88–155. Sage Publications, London

Charlesworth, Sara, and Linda Isherwood. 2021. 'Migrant aged-care workers in Australia: Do they have poorer quality jobs than their locally born counterparts?', *Ageing and Society*, 41:2702–22

Clark, Alison. 2017. 'Unconscious choice: The dissociation of creative animus among writers and psychotherapists.' *Analytical Psychology*, 65(5):710–19

Cleary, Paul. 2021. *Title Fight: How the Yindjibarndi Battled and Defeated a Mining Giant*. Black Inc., Carlton, Vic

Considine, Mark. 2001. *Enterprising States: The Public Management of Welfare-to-Work*. Cambridge University Press, Cambridge

Cooper, Melinda. 2017. *Family Values: Between Neoliberalism and the New Social Conservatism*. Zone Books/MIT Press, Cambridge, MA

—2018. 'Money as punishment: Neoliberal budgetary politics and the fine.' *Australian Feminist Studies*, 33(96):187–208

Curchin, Katherine, Thomas Weight and Alison Ritter. 2021. 'Moral framings in the Australian parliamentary debate on drug testing of welfare recipients.' *Social Policy Administration*. Online first

Cusk, Rachel. 2001. *A Life's Work*. Fourth Estate, London

Dalley, Cameo. 2020. 'The "white card" is grey: Surveillance, endurance and the cashless debit card.' *Australian Journal of Social Issues*, 55(1):51–60

Dickey, Brian. 1992. 'Why were there no poor laws in Australia?' *Journal of Policy History*, 4(2):111–33

Dickinson, Maggie. 2020. *Feeding the Crisis: Care and Abandonment in America's Food Safety Net*. University of California Press, Oakland

Ehrenreich, Barbara. 2001. *Nickel and Dimed: On (Not) Getting By in America*. Metropolitan Books, New York

Ellem, Bradon. 2017. *The Pilbara: From the Deserts Profits Come*. University of Western Australia Publishing, Crawley, WA

Eltham, Ben. 2021. 'A pandemic to die for.' *Meanjin*.

Eubanks, Virginia. 2018. *Automating Inequality: How High-tech Tools Profile, Police and Punish the Poor*. Picador, New York

Fennell, Catherine. 2015. *Last Project Standing: Civics and Sympathy in Post-welfare Chicago*. University of Minnesota Press, Minneapolis

—2016. 'The family toxic: Triaging obligation in post-welfare Chicago.' *South Atlantic Quarterly*, 115(1):9–32

Fisher, Berenice, and Joan Tronto. 1990. 'Toward a feminist theory of caring.' In Emily Abel and Margaret Nelson (eds), *Circles of Care*, pp. 36–54. SUNY Press, Albany, NY

Flanagan, Frances. 2020. 'Imagine us as part of you: Outsourcing and the Serco way.' *Griffith Review*, 67.

Fowkes, Lisa. 2019. *The Application of Income Support Obligations and Penalties to Remote Indigenous Australians, 2013–18*. Centre for Aboriginal Economic Policy Research Working Paper no. 126. Australian National University, Canberra

—2020. 'Seeing people in the computer: The role of information technology in remote employment services.' *Australian Journal of Social Issues*, 55:13–26

Fraser, Nancy and Linda Gordon. 1994. 'A genealogy of dependency: Tracing a keyword of the US welfare state.' *Signs*, 19(2):309–36

Gapps, Stephen. 2018. 'Strike them with terror: April 1816–1817.' In *The Sydney Wars*, pp. 137–54. UNSW Press, Sydney

Gerrard, Jessica, and David Farrugia. 2022. 'Workers in waiting? Work ethic, productive intensities, class and unemployment.' In Steven Threadgold and Jessica Gerrard (eds), *Class in Australia*, pp. 109–24. Monash University Press, Clayton, Vic

Graeber, David. 2012. 'Dead zones of the imagination: On violence, bureaucracy and interpretive labour.' *HAU: Journal of Ethnographic Theory*, 2(2):105–28

—2021. 'After the pandemic, we can't go back to sleep.' *Jacobin*.

Grealy, Liam. 2017. 'Paperless arrests as preventive detention: Motion and documentation in the governance of Indigenous peoples of Australia.' *Sites*, 14(1):80–105

Greenacre, Luke, Skye Akbar, Julie Brimblecombe and Emma McMahon. 2020. 'Income management of government payments on welfare: The Australian cashless debit card.' *Australian Social Work*. Online first

Gregg, Melissa. 2018. *Counterproductive: Time Management in the Knowledge Economy*. Duke University Press, Durham, NC, and London

Haebich, Anna. 2000. *Broken Circles: Fragmenting Indigenous Families, 1800–2000*. Fremantle Arts Centre Press, Fremantle, WA

Harris, Patricia. 1992. 'Penny-pinching activities: Managing poverty under the eye of welfare.' In Kay Saunders and Raymond Evans (eds), *Gender Relations in Australia: Domination and Negotiation*, pp. 287–301. Harcourt Brace Jovanovich, Marrickville, NSW

—2001. 'From relief to mutual obligation: Welfare rationalities and unemployment in 20th-century Australia.' *Journal of Sociology*, 37(5):5–26

Harvey, David. 2005. *A Brief History of Neoliberalism*. Oxford University Press, New York

Hill, David, and T. Carroll. 2003. 'Australia's national tobacco campaign.' *Tobacco Control*, 12:ii9–ii14

Hinkson, Melinda, and Eve Vincent. 2018. 'Shifting Indigenous Australian realities: Dispersal, damage and resurgence.' *Oceania*, 88(3):240–53

Humphrys, Elizabeth. 2018. *How Labour Built Neoliberalism: Australia's Accord, the Labour Movement and the Neoliberal Project*. Brill, The Netherlands

Illi, Elsie. 2019. *Elsie Numitja Illi's Tjukurpa: Elsie's Story*. Ed. Eve Vincent. Published with the assistance of the South Australian History Fund, 2019

Irish, Paul. 2017. *Hidden in Plain View: The Aboriginal People of Coastal Sydney*. New South, Sydney

Jackson, Michael. 1996. 'Introduction.' In Michael Jackson (ed.), *Things as They Are: New Directions in Phenomenological Anthropology*, pp. 1–50. Indiana University Press, Bloomington

Jebb, Mary Anne. 2002. *Blood, Sweat and Welfare*. University of Western Australia Publishing, Crawley, WA

Kingfisher, Catherine, and Michael Goldsmith. 2001. 'Reforming women in the United States and Aotearoa/New Zealand: A comparative ethnography of welfare reform in global context.' *American Anthropologist*, 102(3):714–32

Klein, Elise. 2021. 'Unpaid care, welfare conditionality and expropriation.' *Gender, Work and Organization*, 28(4):1475–89

Klein, Elise, and Sarouche Razi. 2017. *The Cashless Debit Card Trial in the East Kimberley*. Centre for Aboriginal Economic Policy Research, Working Paper no. 121, Australian National University, Canberra

—2018. 'Contemporary tools of dispossession: The cashless debit card trial in the East Kimberley.' *Journal of Australian Political Economy*, 82:84–106

Linebaugh, Peter. 2003. *The London Hanged*. Verso, London and New York

Lea, Tess. 2014. '"From little things, big things grow": The unfurling of wild policy.' *E-flux*, 58

—2020. *Wild Policy: Indigeneity and the Unruly Logics of Intervention*. Stanford University Press, Stanford

Macauley, Wayne. 2019. *Simpson Returns*. Text, Melbourne

McCormack, Karen. 2004. 'Resisting the welfare mother: The power of welfare discourse and tactics of resistance.' *Critical Sociology*, 30(2):355–83

McGann, Michael, Phuc Nguyen and Mark Considine. 2020. 'Welfare conditionality and blaming the unemployed.' *Administration and Society*, 52(3):466–94

McGrath, Anne. 1993. '"Beneath the skin": Australian citizenship, rights and Aboriginal women.' *Journal of Australian Studies*, 17(27):99–114

McGregor, Russell. 1997. *Imagined Destinies: Aboriginal Australians and the Doomed Race Theory, 1880–1939*. Melbourne University Press, Melbourne

McKenzie, Lisa. 2015. *Getting By: Estates, Class and Culture in Austerity Britain*. Policy Press, Bristol

McRobbie, Angela. 2020. *Feminism and the Politics of Resilience: Essays on Gender, Media and the End of Welfare*. Polity, Cambridge, United Kingdom

Maguire, Emily. 2019. *This Is What a Feminist Looks Like*. National Library of Australia Publishing, Canberra

Malcolm, Janet. 2020. *The Silent Woman: Sylvia Plath and Ted Hughes*. Granta, London

Marston, Greg. 2008. 'The war on the poor: Constructing welfare and work in the twenty-first century.' *Critical Discourse Studies*, 5:359–70

Marston, Greg, and Catherine McDonald. 2008. 'Feeling motivated yet? Long-term unemployed people's perspectives on the implementation of workfare in Australia.' *Australian Journal of Social Issues*, 43(2):255–69

Marston, Greg, Louise Humpage, Michelle Peterie, Philip Mendes, Shelley Bielefeld and Zoe Staines. 2022. *Compulsory Income Management in Australia and New Zealand: More Harm Than Good?* Policy Press, Bristol

Martin, David. 2001. *Is Welfare Dependency 'Welfare Poison'? An Assessment of Noel Pearson's Proposals for Aboriginal Welfare Reform*. Centre for Aboriginal Economic Policy, Research discussion paper no. 213. Australian National University, Canberra

Mauss, Marcel. 1990. *The Gift*. Routledge, Great Britain

Mbembe, Achille. 2003. 'Necropolitics.' *Public Culture*, 15(1):11–40

Mead, Lawrence. 1997. 'The rise of paternalism.' In Lawrence Mead (ed.), *The New Paternalism: Supervisory Approaches to Poverty*, pp. 1–38. Brookings Institution Press, Washington, DC

—2000. 'Welfare reform and the family: Lessons from America.' In Peter Saunders (ed.), *Reforming the Australian Welfare State*. Australian Institute of Family Studies, Melbourne.

Meagher, Gabrielle. 2021. 'A genealogy of aged care.' *Arena*, 6

Megalogenis, George. 2019. 'Australasia rising: Who we are becoming.' *Sydney Morning Herald*, 26 January.

Mendes, Philip. 2019. 'Top-down paternalism versus bottom-up community development: A case study of compulsory income management programmes in Australia.' *International Journal of Community and Social Development*, 1(1):42–57

—2020. *Empowerment and Control in the Australian Welfare State: A Critical Analysis of Australian Social Policy Since 1972*. Routledge, New York and London

—2021. 'Conditionalising the unemployed: Why have consecutive Australian governments refused to increase the inadequate Newstart Allowance?' *Australian Journal of Social Issues*, 56:42–53

Mitchell, Emma. 2020. 'Negotiating vulnerability: The experience of long-term social security recipients.' *Sociological Review*, 68(1):225–41

—2022. *Making a Life on Mean Welfare: Voices from Multicultural Sydney*. Policy Press, Bristol

Mitchell, Emma, and Eve Vincent. 2021. 'The shame of welfare? Lived experiences of welfare and culturally inflected experiences of shame.' *Emotion, Space and Society*, 41:1–8

Morris, Barry. 1983. 'From underemployment to unemployment: The changing role of Aborigines in a rural economy.' *Mankind*, 13(6):499–516

—1989. *Domesticating Resistance*. Berg, Oxford and New York

Mounk, Yascha. 2017. *The Age of Responsibility: Luck, Choice and the Welfare State*. Harvard University Press, Cambridge, MA

Murphy, John. 2011. *A Decent Provision: Australian Welfare Policy, 1870 to 1949*. Routledge, Abingdon

—2013. 'Conditional inclusion: Aborigines and welfare rights in Australia, 1900–47.' *Australian Historical Studies*, 44(2):206–26

—Suellen Murray, Jenny Chalmers, Sonia Martin and Greg Marston. 2011. *Half a Citizen: Life on Welfare in Australia*. Allen & Unwin, Sydney

Myers, Fred. 1986. *Pintupi Country, Pintupi Self: Sentiment, Place and Politics among Western Desert Aborigines*. Smithsonian Institute, Washington and London

Needham, Andrew. 2014. 'Sunbelt imperialism: Boosters, Navajos and energy development in the metropolitan southwest.' In Michelle Nickerson and Darren Dochuk (eds), *Sunbelt Rising: The Politics of Space, Place and Region*, pp. 240–64. University of Pennsylvania Press, Philadelphia

Nguyen, Tran, and Selvaraj Velayutham. 2018. 'Street-level discretion, emotional labour and welfare frontline staff at the Australian employment service providers.' *Australian Journal of Social Issues*, 53:158–72

Norman, Heidi. 2015. 'Parramatta and Black Town Native Institutions.' *Dictionary of Sydney*.

—2021. 'Aboriginal worlds and Australian capitalism.' *Labour History*, 121:57–72

O'Brien, Anne. 2008. 'Creating the Aboriginal pauper: Missionary ideas in early 19th-century Australia.' *Social Sciences and Missions*, 21:6–30

—2008. '"Kitchen fragments and garden stuff": Poor Law discourse and Indigenous people in early colonial New South Wales.' *Australian Historical Studies*, 39(2):150–66

O'Connell, Kristin, and Jay Coonan. 2021. 'The effects of Delta on the unemployed.' *Overland*, 26 August

O'Sullivan, Siobhan, Michael McGann and Mark Considine. 2021. *Buying and Selling the Poor: Inside Australia's Welfare-to-Work Market*. Sydney University Press, Sydney

Park, Ruth. 2012. *Swords and Crowns and Rings*. Text Publishing, Melbourne

Pascoe, Bruce. 2014. *Dark Emu*. Magabala Books, Broome

Patrick, Ruth. 2006. 'Living with and responding to the "scrounger" narrative: Exploring everyday strategies of acceptance, resistance and deflection.' *Journal of Poverty and Social Justice*, 24(3):245–59

Pearson, Luke. 2018. 'Tony Abbott and the white man's burden.' *IndigenousX*. https://indigenousx.com.au/tony-abbott-and-the-white-mans-burden

Pearson, Noel. 2000. 'Passive welfare and the destruction of Indigenous society in Australia.' In Peter Saunders (ed.), *Reforming the Australian Welfare State*. Australian Institute of Family Studies, Melbourne.

—2009. 'Our right to take responsibility.' In *Up from the Mission: Selected Writings*, pp. 143–71. Black Inc., Melbourne

Peel, Mark. 2003. *The Lowest Rung: Voices of Australian Poverty*. Cambridge University Press, Cambridge, UK

Peterie, Michelle, Greg Marston and Louise Humpage. 2021. 'The trope of the vulnerable child in conditional welfare discourses: An Australian case study.' *Journal of Sociology*. Online first

Peterie, Michelle, Gaby Ramia, Greg Marston and Roger Patulny. 2019. 'Emotional compliance and emotion as resistance: Shame and anger among the long-term unemployed.' *Work, Employment and Society*, 33(5):794–811

Peterson, Nicolas. 1993. 'Demand sharing: Reciprocity and the pressure for generosity among foragers.' *American Anthropologist*, 95(4):860–74

Povinelli, Elizabeth. 1993. *Labor's Lot: The Power, History and Culture of Aboriginal Action*. University of Chicago Press, Chicago

Rothwell, Nicolas. 2008. 'Indigenous insiders chart an end to victimhood.' *Australian Literary Review*, 3(8):1, 15–16

Rowse, Tim. 2002. 'McClure's "mutual obligation" and Pearson's "reciprocity": Can they be reconciled?' *Australian Journal of Social Issues*, 37(3):263–76

Scambary, Benedict. 2013. *My Country, Mine Country: Indigenous People, Mining and Development Contestation in Remote Australia*. Centre for Aboriginal Economic Policy Research, Canberra

Schram, Sanford, Joe Soss, Richard C. Fording and Linda Houser. 2009. 'Deciding to discipline: Race, choice and punishment at the frontlines of welfare reform.' *American Sociological Review*, 74(3):398–422

Sennett, Richard. 2003. *Respect in a World of Inequality*. W.W. Norton, New York

Sennett, Richard, and Jonathan Cobb. 1993. *The Hidden Injuries of Class*. W.W. Norton & Company, London and New York

Sheppard, Jill, and Nicholas Biddle. 2017. 'Class, capital and identity in Australian society.' *Australian Journal of Political Science*, 52(4):500–16

Shildrick, Tracy, and Robert MacDonald. 2013. 'Poverty talk: How people experiencing poverty deny their poverty and why they blame "the poor".' *Sociological Review*, 61(2):285–303

Silverstein, Ben, and Claire McLisky. 2018. 'Rethinking paternalism: From nineteenth-century Aboriginal missions to contemporary neoliberal policy.' In Ben Silverstein (ed.), *Conflict, Adaptation, Transformation: Richard Broome and the Practice of Aboriginal History*, pp. 38–62. Aboriginal Studies Press, Canberra

Simmonds, Alecia. 2021. 'Troubled minds.' *Inside Story*.

Skyring, Fiona. 2012. 'Low wages, low rents and pension cheques: The introduction of equal wages in the Kimberley, 1968–1969.' In Natasha Fijn, Ian Keen, Christopher Lloyd and Michael Pickering (eds), *Indigenous Participation in Australian Economies II: Historical Engagements and Current Enterprises*, pp. 153–69. ANU Press, Canberra

Soldatić, Karen. 2011. 'Appointment time: Disability and neoliberal workfare temporalities.' *Critical Sociology*, 39(3):405–19

Soldatić, Karen, and Barbara Pini. 2009. 'The three Ds of welfare reform: Disability, disgust and deservingness.' *Australian Journal of Human Rights*, 15(1):77–95

Soldatić, Karen, Kelly Somers, Kim Spurway and Georgia van Toorn. 2017. 'Emplacing indigeneity and rurality in neoliberal disability welfare reform: The lived experience of Aboriginal people with disabilities in the West Kimberley, Australia.' *Environment and Planning A*, 49(10):2342–61

Spies-Butcher, Ben. 2014. 'Marketisation and the dual welfare state: Neoliberalism and inequality in Australia.' *Economic and Labour Relations Review*, 25(2):185–201

Stead, Victoria. 2021. 'Precarity's reach: Intersections of history, life and labour in the Australian horticultural industry.' *Journal of the Royal Anthropological Institute*, 27(2):303–20

Strakosch, Elizabeth. 2015. *Neoliberal Indigenous Policy: Settler Colonialism and the 'Post-welfare' State*. Palgrave Macmillan, London

Swain, Shurlee. 2007. 'Writing the history of women and welfare.' *Australian Feminist Studies*, 22(52):43–7

Swain, Tony, and Gary Trompf. 1995. 'Tradition.' In *The Religions of Oceania*, pp. 18–45. Routledge, London and New York

Symons, Michael. 2007. *One Continuous Picnic*. Melbourne University Press, Melbourne

Taylor, Barbara. 2015. *The Last Asylum: A Memoir of Madness in Our Times*. Penguin Random House, United Kingdom

Taylor, David, Matthew Gray and David Stanton. 2016. 'New conditionality in Australian social security policy.' *Australian Journal of Social Issues*, 51(1):3–26

Tumarkin, Maria. 2018. *Axiomatic*. Brow Books, Melbourne

Veracini, Lorenzo. 2010. *Settler Colonialism: A Theoretical Overview*. Palgrave Macmillan, Basingstoke

Vuong, Ocean. 2019. *On Earth We're Briefly Gorgeous*. Jonathan Cape, London

Wacquant, Loïc. 2009. *Punishing the Poor: The Neoliberal Government of Insecurity*. Duke University Press, Durham, NC

Warin, Megan, Tanya Zivkovic, Vivienne Moore, Paul R. Ward and Michelle Jones. 2015. 'Short horizons and obesity futures: Disjunctures between public health interventions and everyday temporalities.' *Social Science and Medicine*, 128:309–15

Watson, Irene. 2014. 'In the Northern Territory intervention, what is saved or rescued and at what cost?' In Timothy Neal, Crystal McKinnon and Eve Vincent (eds), *History, Power, Text*, pp. 167–86. UTS E-Press, Sydney

Watson, Nicole. 2011. 'The Northern Territory Emergency Response—Has it really improved the lives of Aboriginal women and children?' *Australian Feminist Law Journal*, 35(1):147–63

Watt, Elizabeth. 2018. 'Pearson's mission: Revisiting Noel Pearson's revisionist history of Hope Vale.' *Journal of Australian Studies*, 42(1):34–50

—2020. 'Is the BasicsCard "shaming" Aboriginal people? Exploring the differing responses to welfare quarantining in Cape York.' *Australian Journal of Social Issues*, 55(1):40–50

Watts, Rob. 1982. 'The origins of the Australian welfare state.' In Richard Kennedy (ed.), *Australian Welfare History: Critical Essays*, pp. 225–55. Macmillan, South Melbourne

Weber, Max. 2003. *The Protestant Ethic and the Spirit of Capitalism*. Dover Publications, Mineola, NY

—2006. 'Bureaucracy.' In Aradhana Sharma and Akhil Gupta (eds), *The Anthropology of the State*, pp. 49–70. Blackwell Publishing, Malden, MA

White, John. 2010. 'Peas, beans and riverbanks: Seasonal picking and dependence in the Tuross Valley.' In Ian Keen (ed.), *Indigenous Participation in Australian Economies: Historical and Anthropological Perspectives*, pp. 109–26. ANU Press, Canberra

Whittaker, Alison. 2018. *Blakwork*. Magabala Books, Broome

Winnicott, Donald. 1965. *The Maturational Processes and the Facilitating Environment*. International Universities Press, New York

—2005. *Playing and Reality*. Routledge Classics, Abingdon

Wright, Alexis. 1997. *Grog War*. Magabala Books, Broome

Wynhausen, Elisabeth. 2005. *Dirt Cheap*. Pan Macmillan, Sydney

Yeatman, Anna. 2000. 'Mutual obligation: What kind of contract is this?' In Peter Saunders (ed.), *Reforming the Australian Welfare State*. Australian Institute of Family Studies, Melbourne.

Young, Diana. 2010. 'Dingo scalping and the frontier economy in the north-west of South Australia.' In Ian Keen (ed.), *Indigenous Participation in Australian Economies: Historical and Anthropological Perspectives*, pp. 91–108. ANU Press, Canberra

Index

Abbott Coalition government 39, 45
Aboriginal people
  citizenship rights 94–5
  eligibility for social security payments 28–9, 34
  erasure of labour 42
  frontier violence 23
  ineligibility for age pensions 25
  involvement in settler economies 30–2
  poverty 33
  precarious, unpredictable labour 32–3
  redistribution of resources 119
  relations twentieth-century welfare state 27–8
  shame 93–4, 106–7
  treatment in nineteenth century 23–4
  See also First Nations people; Indigenous policy; *names* of peoples or language groups
age pensions 24–5, 30
aged-care institutions 115–16
aged-care workers 114–15
Albanese, Anthony 128–9
Albanese Labor government xi, 71, 129–30
Anangu, dingo scalp trade 31
anthropology 16–18
Appin massacre 23
Arthur, Jay 107
asylum system 117–18
Australian welfare state
  digital transformation 13–14
  disciplinary turn 13
  dual welfare state 39–40
  emergence 27
  gender dynamics 131
  history 12–14
  middle-class welfare 40
  mutual obligation 37–8, 41
  privatisation of social service delivery 14, 36–7
  shift to bureaucratic models of assistance 27
  uncaring policy architecture 131
  wage earner's welfare state 25–6
autonomy, dependency and 123–4

Baak, Melanie 107
BasicsCard 43–4, 46, 47, 55
Benevolent Society of New South Wales 23
biographies, rewritten to fit a policy narrative 91–3
Brady, Michelle 78
Buckland, Ella 9, 11, 15
Bundaberg–Hervey Bay, Qld, cashless debit card trial 46, 57, 69, 72
Burke, Tony 114

Cadigal people 21, 30
Cape York
  BasicsCard 43, 108
  cashless debit card 72
  Hope Vale mission 41
  impact of welfare 40–1
  income management 43, 72
Cape York Welfare Reform Trial 43
care, definition x, 111
care responsibilities, of social security recipients 15–16, 19–20
caregiving x
  as invisible work 111
  parenting of dependants 119–24
  physical work and emotional effort of 111–12
  providing protective presence to another 119
  by welfare recipients 19–20, 131–2
Carer Payment 4, 112
case managers 38, 74, 75, 78, 83, 85–8, 90–1, 104, 124–7
Casey, Simone 78

INDEX

cashless debit card
  abolition 72, 129–30
  aims 4, 47, 67, 71, 112
  breaching of conditions 48
  in Bundaberg–Hervey Bay 46, 57, 69, 72
  in Cape York 72
  in Ceduna. *See* Ceduna cashless debit card trial
  difference to BasicsCard 46
  in East Kimberley region 5, 46, 56, 72
  evaluations of impact 64, 69–72, 140n26
  exemptions 66–7, 100–1
  in Goldfields 46, 57
  issue and administration of 14
  in Northern Territory 72
  origins of 44, 45, 54
  percentage of Indigenous recipients 4–5
  research into 6–8
  targets 52, 69
  as top-down process 55
  trials 9, 46–7, 56–7, 71–2
  wellbeing exemptions 66–7, 100
  racism 95
Ceduna cashless debit card trial 100–1
  anxiety and stress experienced by recipients 58, 60–1, 95–6
  consultation before implementation 52–3
  duration of trial 56–7
  evaluation of impacts 63–5, 70–1, 140n26
  exemptions 66–7, 100–1
  financial responsibility exemptions 100–1
  fungibility 63–4
  inclusion of Yalata 5
  income support payments covered 7
  infantilisation and demeaning of recipients 112
  initial reactions of recipients to receipt of card 51
  introduction of trial 4, 46, 52–3, 56
  issue and administration of 14, 61–2
  media reports 52–3
  missing money from accounts 61–2
  names given to card by community 52
  non-Indigenous recipients 59
  operation 4, 7
  opposition to implementation 52, 55–6
  percentage of Indigenous recipients 5, 59
  practical problems of using 60–1
  purpose according to recipients 4
  shame experienced by recipients 93–4, 95–6, 106
  strategies to get around conditions 67–9
  target population 52
  variation of terms 101–3
  wellbeing exemptions 66–7, 100
Ceduna reserve 32
Ceduna, SA
  1967 referendum results 95
  alcohol and drug problems 52, 58, 59
  Community Panels 101–3
  grassroots political possibilities 55
charitable institutions 22–3, 24
child endowment payments 27, 28
childcare subsidies 40
Clinton administration 38
colonial gaze 16
Commonwealth Employment Service (CES) 37
Community Development Employment Projects scheme (CDEP) 57–8
Community Development Program (CDP) 37
conditional welfare 47–8, 88, 120, 121, 129, 130
consultation in political life 52–5
COVID supplement ix, xi, 6
COVID-19 pandemic ix–x, 20, 111, 114
Cusk, Rachel 121

deindustrialisation 34
deinstitutionalisation 118
dependency
  and autonomy 123–4
  critique of 117–18, 123
  as individual character trait 117

INDEX

negative connotations 116, 117
possibilities of accepting 123–7
shifting cultural associations over time 116–17
as social relationship 116–17
welfare dependence 35–6, 91, 92, 97, 116, 117, 118–19
Depression 26–7
dingo scalp trade 31
Disability Support Pension 4, 7, 83, 90, 122, 126, 128, 129
distancing narratives 89
Dodson, Patrick 46
Dole 26
dole 'bludgers' 35, 118

East Kimberley region, WA, cashless debit card trial 5, 46, 64, 70
Ehrenreich, Barbara 110
Ellery, Maryanne 128
employment services, Workforce Australia 13–14
ethnography 15, 18–19

Family Responsibility Commission (FRC) 43
Family Tax Benefit 40
Far West Community Heads Group 52
First Nations people
living conditions in remote areas 10
orientation to relations among kin 109
state control over 11
See also Aboriginal people; Indigenous policy; Torres Strait Islanders
Forrest, Andrew 'Twiggy' 44, 45, 54
The Forrest Review: Creating Parity 45, 52, 54
Fortescue Metals Group (FMG) 45
frontier violence 23

Goldfields cashless debit card trial, WA 46, 57, 70
Graeber, David 20
Guugu Yimidhirr people 108

Harvester judgment 25, 32
Haynes, Mick 52
Healthy Welfare Card 45, 54

Hervey Bay cashless debit card trial, Qld 46, 57, 69
Hope Vale mission 41
Howard Coalition government 37, 42–3

Illi, Elsie Numitja (Pitjantjatjara woman) 10–11, 31, 131–2
income management
in Cape York 43
compulsory income management 42–3
in Northern Territory 43
pre-emptive enforcement of conditions 47
income management tools 13
income support payments 3–4, 89–90
income tax system 17
independence
total independence as fantasy 127
valorisation of 117, 118
India 13
Indigenous policy
assimilation 27–8
state-based protection regimes 24
Indue 14, 61–2
inequality, geographical distribution 58
inflation 34
intergenerational welfare dependency 91, 92
interviewees (pseudonyms)
Aero 65–7, 100
Anna 75, 81, 113, 118, 124
Anne 101
Arlie 90–1, 122
Aunty Vera 7, 8, 31
Ayesha 35, 76–7, 91–2, 104, 105, 122
Bec 124–7, 130
Brian 96
Chazzy 62
Ciara 77
Craig 51, 100
Dustin 57–8, 98, 102
Elena 69
Ella 86–7 113–14
Eloise 10 76, 80, 83–4, 92, 105–6
Gladys 63 111–12, 132
Helen 60 102–3
Jo 86, 88
June 57, 68, 112–13

Kelli-Anne 60–1
Kieran 63
Kylie 82–3, 84, 119
Lallie 87–8, 120–1
Lauris 81–2, 119
Lefa 76, 120
Maude 3, 4–5, 16, 19–20, 106
Megan 98–100, 104, 120, 130
Misha 80, 86
Natasha 3, 9–10, 11–12, 80, 119, 122, 123, 132
Pam 54–5, 71
Rex 59
Robby 21, 32, 51, 93, 94, 95, 96
Rose 102
Shelby 79, 91, 104, 105
Stacey 60, 95–6
Stan 93–4
Stephanie 97
Svetlana 73–5, 80, 86, 120, 121–2, 131
Trish 78, 105, 130
Tynisha 63
Uncle Bert 8, 28–9, 31
Uncle Clive 60
Valerie 3, 4, 17
interviews
 locations 80–1
 phone interviews 81

JobSeeker ix, xi, 6, 7, 77, 90, 126
Julalikari Council 140n13

Koonibba mission 31, 94

labour movement 22
Learner Driver Mentor program 7, 133n8

Macquarie, Lachlan 23
McCormack, Karen 108
McGrath, Ann 28, 29
Mead, Lawrence 35–6
mean welfare 38
Menzies government 27, 28
migrants, as undeserving 89
minimum wage standard 25–6
mining boom 44
mining welfare 45

missions 31, 41, 94
Mitchell, Emma 97
Morrison Coalition government xi, 39, 46–7, 72
mutual obligation 9, 37–8, 41, 47–8
mutual obligation failures 121–2

Native Institution, Parramatta 23
Navajo people 44
neoliberalism 14, 34, 118
new paternalism 35–6, 47
New Poor Law 1834 (England) 22
Northern Territory
 BasicsCard 42–3
 cashless debit card 72
 compulsory income management 42–3, 72
Northern Territory Intervention 42–3
nuclear family, normalisation of 25

old age pensions 24–5, 30
'ologist' [poem] (Whittaker) 16
ORIMA Research, evaluation of cashless debit card 64, 70

parenting
 devaluing of work involved in 131
 time required for 120–1
Parenting Payment 5, 7
Parenting Payment (Single) 4, 5, 34, 74, 130
ParentsNext
 acceptable activities 75, 78–9, 87
 administration and delivery of program 14–15, 73–4, 75–6, 82, 86, 113–14
 aims 73, 79
 anxiety felt by participants 103–5
 compliance requirements 12, 121–3, 130
 compulsory participation 130
 costs of participation 82–3, 105
 eligibility for 73, 75–7, 79–80, 86–7
 evaluation by participants 81–3, 119
 exemptions from 75, 104
 Indigenous participants 79
 individual compliance system 47
 initial phone calls 73, 75–7, 91
 intensive streams 79

introduction and rollout 5
number of participants 8
number of single parents 8
number of women participants 8
participant–adviser interactions 74, 78, 85–8, 90–1, 104
Participation Fund 79
participation plans 74, 81, 83, 87, 104, 123, 125, 130
precursor to 78
reclassification of parents as unemployed 78, 131
reporting requirements 74, 79, 104–5, 130
research into 8–10, 80–1
Senate inquiry into 9, 122–3
suspension of payments 9–10, 74, 75, 79, 80, 121, 131
working women as ideal mothers 6, 36
passive welfare 41
pastoral industry 29
paternalism
new paternalism 35–6, 47
Noel Pearson's conception of 41–2
Patrick, Rex 46–7
pearling industry 30–1
Pearson, Luke 59
Pearson, Noel 40–2
philanthropy, nature of 25
Pilbara region 44
Pitjantjatjara-speakers 5, 7, 10–11, 19, 31, 106, 109, 131
policy co-design 53–5
Poor Law thinking 24
poor laws 22, 89
poverty
Aboriginal people 32–3
deserving versus undeserving poor 23, 89
in Georgian England 21–2
single-parent families 77, 113
public housing 128
punitive welfare 47

Queensland
Bundaberg–Hervey Bay cashless debit card trial 46, 57, 69, 72
See also Cape York

Racial Discrimination Act 1975 (Cth) 34, 43
racism 88, 95
Ramsey, Rowan 64
Redfern 31
refugees, as undeserving 89
relief work 26–7
Rishworth, Amanda 72, 129–30
Robodebt 13, 39

self-advocacy 88
self-identity, shame and 97
Sennett, Richard 88, 96, 97–8, 117, 123
Serco 76
shame
and self-identity 97
and welfare 93–4, 95–8, 106–9
single motherhood
attacks on Black single mothers in US 116, 117
restrictions choices on welfare recipients 106
stigmatisation of 98–100, 105–6, 118
single-mother families
with more than three children 118
percentage of one-parent families 77
single-parent families, poverty 77, 113
smoking 17
social security payments
Aboriginal eligibility for 28–9, 34
eligibility for 27
rates xi
stigma attached to 26
suspension of 9–10, 37
See also specific payments
South Africa 13
South Australia. *See* Ceduna cashless debit card; Ceduna, SA

Targeted Compliance Framework 9, 121
tax concessions 40
taxpayers, versus welfare recipients 17, 35, 89
Taylor, Barbara 117–18
Torres Strait Islanders 30–1
Tudge, Alan 55–6
Turnbull, Malcolm 56

unemployed people, public censure of 90
unemployment 34, 35
Unemployment and Sickness Benefits Act 1944 (Cth) 27
United Kingdom
  attacks on migrants as undeserving 89
  distancing narratives 89
  poor laws 22
  poverty in Georgian England 21–2
  Universal Credit system 13
  welfare state retrenchment 38–9
United States
  attacks on Black single mothers 116, 117
  destitution of Navajo people 44
  welfare reforms under Clinton administration 38
  welfare spending 138n25
  welfare stigma 108

Vuong, Ocean 110

wage earner's welfare state 25–6
Wallaga Lake reserve 30
Watt, Elizabeth 108
welfare dependence 116, 117, 118–19
welfare dependency 35–6, 91, 92, 97
welfare fraud 39
welfare recipients
  caregiving by 19–20, 131–2
  categorisation of people as 15, 17
  drug-testing of 39

  shame 93–4, 95–8, 106–9
  stereotypes 118–19
  versus taxpayers 17, 35, 89
welfare spending, percentage of annual budget 34
welfare state. *See* Australian welfare state
Welfare to Work policy 78
West Coast Sentinel 53
Western Australia
  East Kimberley cashless debit card trial 5, 46, 56, 72
  Goldfields cashless debit card trial 46, 57, 70
White Australia Policy 24
Whitlam Labor government 34
Whittaker, Alison 16
Winnicott, Donald 123–4, 126
work
  aged-care work 114
  definition 42
  dignity of 97
  invisible work 100–11
  waged care work 112, 113, 114
Work for the Dole 37, 47, 98
Workforce Australia 13–14
workhouses 22
work-shy 'bludgers' 90
Wynhausen, Elisabeth 110

Yankunytjatjara-speakers 31
Yindjibarndi Aboriginal Corporation (YAC) 45
Yuin people 30